Cambridge

C000292923

Elements in Critical...

edite...

Kristian Kristiansen, *Un... ..., Gothenburg*

Michael Rowlands, *UCL*

Francis Nyamnjoh, *University of Cape Town*

Astrid Swenson, *Bath University*

Shu-Li Wang, *Academia Sinica*

Ola Wetterberg, *University of Gothenburg*

GLOBAL HERITAGE, RELIGION, AND SECULARISM

Trinidad Rico
Rutgers University

CAMBRIDGE
UNIVERSITY PRESS

CAMBRIDGE
UNIVERSITY PRESS

University Printing House, Cambridge CB2 8BS, United Kingdom

One Liberty Plaza, 20th Floor, New York, NY 10006, USA

477 Williamstown Road, Port Melbourne, VIC 3207, Australia

314–321, 3rd Floor, Plot 3, Splendor Forum, Jasola District Centre, New Delhi – 110025, India

103 Penang Road, #05–06/07, Visioncrest Commercial, Singapore 238467

Cambridge University Press is part of the University of Cambridge.

It furthers the University's mission by disseminating knowledge in the pursuit of education, learning, and research at the highest international levels of excellence.

www.cambridge.org
Information on this title: www.cambridge.org/9781009183598
DOI: 10.1017/9781009183581

First published 2021

A catalogue record for this publication is available from the British Library.

ISBN 978-1-009-18359-8 Paperback
ISSN 2632-7074 (online)
ISSN 2632-7066 (print)

Cambridge University Press has no responsibility for the persistence or accuracy of URLs for external or third-party internet websites referred to in this publication and does not guarantee that any content on such websites is, or will remain, accurate or appropriate.

Global Heritage, Religion, and Secularism

Elements in Critical Heritage Studies

DOI: 10.1017/9781009183581
First published online: December 2021

Trinidad Rico
Rutgers University
Author for correspondence: Trinidad Rico, Trinidad.rico@rutgers.edu

Abstract: Religion and spirituality have been scarcely addressed in heritage preservation history, discourse, and practice. More recently, increased interest in the intersections between the study of religion and heritage preservation in both academic studies and institutional initiatives highlights obstacles that the field has yet to overcome theoretically and methodologically. This Element surveys the convergences of religious and heritage traditions. It argues that the critical heritage turn has not adequately considered the legacy of secularism that underpins the history and contemporary practices of heritage preservation. This omission is what has left the field of heritage studies ill-equipped to support the study and management of a heritage of religion broadly construed.

Keywords: heritage, religion, secularism, sacred, expertise

ISBNs: 9781009183598 (PB), 9781009183581 (OC)
ISSNs: 2632-7074 (online), 2632-7066 (print)

Contents

1 The Heritage Cult

Religion currently figures within heritage preservation history, discourse, and practice primarily through the interrelated ideas of a "heritagization of the sacred" and a "sacralization of heritage," two ways in which heritage and religion have been made to converge. However, scholars in critical heritage studies have argued that the institutionalized heritage discourse that forms the backbone of contemporary studies in heritage and preservation does not adequately represent or incorporate religious discourse, traditions, or steward-ship (Karlström, 2013; Byrne, 2014). The use of outstanding or universal heritage value as a neutral arbiter in conflicting interpretations and management strategies for historic sites of religious nature further complicates, rather than resolves, these tensions.

Advocates for a critical turn in heritage studies have discussed extensively the ways in which practices of preservation are rooted in Western ideologies of objectification and rationalism based on secular values (Smith, 2006; Harrison, 2013; Byrne, 2014; Rico, 2019). Operationally, global heritage institutions such as the United Nations Educational, Scientific and Cultural Organization (UNESCO) and its supporting organizations have recognized to some extent the difficulty of representing religious traditions in their work (Bumbaru, 2008). Some anthropologists have deemed the challenge so insurmountable that they have called for the exclusion of "the spirits" from heritage programs (Berliner, 2013). Such a view echoes earlier calls to delegitimize studies of heritage that center on "the intangible" (Baillie and Chippindale, 2007).

This Element confronts religion as an outcast in heritage studies, examining what Anna Karlström calls a "structural problem" (2013) within heritage discourse. Ubiquitous in the history of heritage and its preservation across the world, this problem has produced tensions and conflicts surrounding the aims of preservation as they relate to the integrity and well-being of religious practices, ultimately stymieing the field's ability to engage productively with religious discourses. Thus far, the examination of religion has had a privileged but restricted place in the historiography of heritage and preservation studies. It is mobilized most visibly and intentionally in debates that seek to make sense of the dialogics of preservation and destruction (Schildgen, 2008; Harrison, 2013), signaling a dominant positioning of religion within the context of a conflict of values. However, in other disciplinary debates that address the same ontological encounters, the theme of coexistence is elaborated along a heritage of tolerance (Bigelow, 2010: 5), underscoring instead the political choreographies that activate conflict and coexistence around sacred sites (Barkan and Barkey, 2015). While anthropologists Christophe Brumann and David Berliner conceptualize a heritage that "often serves to render harmless the potentially disruptive nature of religious sites" (2016: 25), scholars of religion seek to better understand the ways in which heritage discourse enforces a reclassification of religious value that allows secular – and, therefore, contested – governance (e.g. Rots, 2019). These diametrically opposed views raise the question: To what extent does heritage discourse itself propel and weaponize such disagreements? Answering requires historicizing and contextualizing an international heritage discourse that operates as a catalyst for, moderator of, and aggressor in the production of tensions between "heritage values" and "religious values" in different cultural and political contexts.

The tensions surrounding religion and religious sites that feature prominently in heritage and preservation literature include (1) tensions over interpretations and uses of historic resources by different religious traditions and (2) tensions between religious and secular management strategies. In both cases, global heritage discourse (and its experts) appears to overlook its operation as a competing ontological reality. However, a rich debate around the material dimensions of religious practice alludes to the role of heritage discourse and practice in mobilizing processes of sacralization and secularization that confront the legitimate authority of religious objects and performances (Meyer and de Witte, 2013). Through a historical survey, this Element brings to the foreground the forces of secularism attached to global heritage discourses. This Element also discusses the ways in which heritage preservation has mobilized and institutionalized its own sacrality in the search for effective consensus and collaboration. It therefore examines global heritage discourse as a disruptive force in the study and assimilation of a heritage of religion into the tropes of global heritage. By exploring how leading and influential heritage institutions and their instruments engage with religious thought, this Element proposes a much broader framework of examination.

More specifically, this Element positions "heritage and religion" as a historically, politically, and socioculturally contingent relationship. The other related scale embedded in this discussion is the circulation of heritage *as* religion, that is, as a set of ideas and actions that circulate effectively through specific doctrinal documents and forms of expertise. These distinct and deliberate recombinations aim to disrupt "proprietary claims and a relation of encompassment" (Lincoln, 1996: 225), which has seen religious discourse primarily addressed from and translated into a heritage preservation ideology via the field of heritage studies rather than on more ontologically neutral grounds. The goal, in other words, is to address the interrelation of heritage and religion from a more critical and reflexive middle ground. This engagement also recognizes its own destabilizing effects. As in the study of the history of religions, this ontological encounter sees a subject matter dominated by temporal, contextual, situated, human, and material dimensions (in this case, heritage value) examined in a context that represents itself as eternal, transcendent, spiritual, and divine (cf. Lincoln, 1996).

In the foundational text *The Heritage Crusade and the Spoils of History*, David Lowenthal (1998) calls attention to the circulation of a pervasive religious analogy that aligns with the operation of heritage preservation as a popular faith. Discursively, he traces the first known use of the term "heritage" in the Western canon to a biblical origin in Psalm 16's "goodly heritage" (Lowenthal, 1998: xiii), but the modern "cult of heritage," he writes, is likened by its devotees to a spiritual calling. While his rhetoric denotes a certain bias against religion itself and does not elaborate further on the markers of cultism that would justify this characterization, I would argue that this comparison is not unfounded or isolated. Heritage preservation discourse, in fact, is rife with religious and spiritual metaphors. Discussions about the authenticity of heritage objects as an intangible yet powerful quality are articulated through the appreciation of an "aura" (cf. Benjamin, 1992 [1936]; see Holtorf and Schadla-Hall, 1999). In addition, the conceptualization of the unique and complex network of significance that creates and sustains heritage value is articulated as the existence of a genius loci, a "spirit of place" (ICOMOS, 2008a), namely their living, social, and spiritual nature. The cult analogy is common, in large part enabled by the way in which aesthetics and affect are used to win hearts and minds in both religious and preservation discourses (Hall, 2011: 6). In his work from the 1970s, Yi-Fu Tuan (1989) refers to the preservation of historic buildings and the establishment of museums as "the cult of the past" that has little in common with cultural rootedness. More recently, Cristoph Rausch (2017) goes as far as proposing an epiphanic moment for this cult under the auspices of UNESCO: the International Campaign to Save the Monuments of Nubia associated with the construction of the Aswan High Dam in Egypt. The rise of the cult, in this sense, aligns with the internationalization of heritage discourse and practice and the widespread acceptance of a universal notion of global heritage (cf. Meskell, 2018).

The metaphor of heritage preservation as a cult can be traced to earlier writings in the field that use the term with different connotations that are not necessarily implying a small, sinister, or obsessive uncritical belief. Alois Riegl (1982) christened the era of heritage preservation as the rise of a "cult of monuments," which defined a growing interest in the preservation of artistic and historic monuments in German-speaking Europe at the time. His work was then expanded to examine preservation through the analytical lens of an "age value" in the work of art, a value that produces a quasi-religious experience.

Conservator Matthew Hayes argues that "it is tempting to recognize an evoca-tion of the worship of art so pervasive at the time . . . still, this should not ignore the difficulty of the term *Kultus,* somewhat lost in translation as *The modern cult of monuments.* From the Latin *colere,* the word meant veneration, but also care or cultivation" (2019: 138). Hayes (2019) argues that while *colere* may signify religion and shares the same root as the word "culture," Riegl often uses the term in less mystical ways to refer to reverence or appreciation. Nevertheless, the call to arms that has since given the heritage and preservation field its spiritual undertones can be related to Riegl's proposition of age value as an appealing and inclusive category that is "based on emotion rather than intellect" (Lamprakos, 2014: 423).

These tensions between reason and emotion run deep in the historical emer-gence and contemporary practices of heritage preservation and have an effect on the ability of institutionalized heritage preservation discourses to interact with and encompass religious discourse. It could be argued that the alignment of heritage preservation discourse with discourses of sacrality denies the role of reason in the service of specific agendas. For example, it is a discourse that reinforces the idea that heritage preservationism follows a mode of belief that relies on revealed faith rather than rational proof (Lowenthal, 1998: 2). As such, it strategically empowers the two main types of voices of authority in heritage preservation. For experts, actual or potential "heritage sacredness" codifies a preferential understanding of heritage value that is hard to ascertain without specialized expertise. Other interest groups mobilize sacrality, an elusive qual-ity used to claim exclusive access to property by calling on a type of value that may be secret or intimate and, therefore, impossible to rationalize by said heritage experts (Lowenthal, 1998: 236).

Lowenthal, who is credited as a key analyst of the pillars of heritage preser-vation thought, puts forth a religious analogy for the purposes of centering heritage discourse along the operation of rationality. His review of the mobil-ization of presumed heritage sacredness, drawing on Anglo-American and Euro-centered preservation practices and debates, concludes that churches, cathedrals, and religious art were stewarded less as sacred legacies than as objects of national pride and secular profit (Lowenthal, 1998: 61). Some architects and museum scholars might disagree. Drawing on Le Corbusier's idea of *the ineffable,* that is, the unutterable, contemporary scholars and practi-tioners in architectural design argue that religious buildings and sacred land-scapes "often contribute in critical ways to shaping the larger cultural and urban fabric of contemporary life" (Britton, 2010: 10). Therefore, the concept that architectural and religious experiences share a common language and can enrich each other (Goldberg, 2010) idealizes an approach to the preservation of heritage resources *as* religious material resources and, certainly, proposes a desirable and attainable overlapping practice. Such a possibility gains momentum in the idea of the museum as sacred space. Architectural critic Paul Goldberger suggests that "we" (presumably, the "West") have "conflated the aesthetic and the sacred, which is why … the art museum seems to have replaced the cathedral" (2010: 6). Gretchen Buggeln suggests that the rational Enlightenment thought that accompanied the rise of eighteenth-century museums navigated the divide between knowledge and faith by appropriating the ritual atmosphere and the language of the sacred to channel a transformative experience for the visitor (2012: 36–37). Deliberately designed to resemble older ceremonial monuments and temples until the mid-twentieth century, the museum can be easily translated into a ritual space that invites ritual performance, a space where religious experiences like revelation, transcendence, and transformation can be enacted secularly (Duncan, 1995: 2, 9, 10). This aligns with the invention of aesthetics as a transference of spiritual values from the sacred realm into secular time and space (Duncan, 1995: 14). The way in which Enlightenment rationality found a surrogate ritual atmosphere in the institution of the museum inspires an examination of the parallel ways in which heritage discourse was crafted to offer a similar ritual surrogate.

1.1 From Cult to Culture

Scholars in the critical turn in heritage studies have been skeptical of the utility of perpetuating the heritage-as-cult analogy, problematizing instead genealogies, agencies, and practices that enable or disable the discourses and forms of authority that can be associated with religious significance. For example, focusing on a *patrimonial regime* as a force of meaning-making, Valdimar Hafstein (2018) asserts that the religious analogy is overblown, favoring instead an analogy with environmental movements. His work seeks to explore more specific ways in which the regime cultivates responsible subjects (Hafstein and Skrydstrup, 2020). Meanwhile, Kathryn Lafrenz Samuels proposes to move the study of heritage "from cult to culture" (2018: 20) in order to bring a spotlight to the *cultural* part of the term "cultural heritage" and, thus, re-center heritage studies within an anthropological tradition. Addressing more specifically the place of a heritage of faith in global heritage, Britta Rudolff refers to the postmodern cult of values as signaling a shift from an objectivist to a subjectivist field that pivots on the fall of authenticity as an absolute standard for preservation (2006: 57, 2010: 72).

These separate yet coherent calls for aligning the study of heritage and preservation to the politics of knowledge production for cultural heritage represent a promising intervention. They contextualize *heritagization* as a transformation operating within social processes that mobilize sacralization as a political-aesthetic practice (Meyer and de Witte, 2013: 280). Therefore, it is worth preserving the analytical idea of a "heritage cult" for various reasons while also continuing to flesh out how this metaphor can facilitate critical praxis. First, heritage discourse and preservation practices are circulated as a form of religion in the Geertzian sense: a system of symbols that acts to establish powerful, pervasive, and long-lasting moods and motivations (Geertz, 1966). This is precisely the fundamentalism of heritage preservation, which dictates that all other value hierarchies fold into those of preservationists. Therefore, rather than fetishizing heritage discourse as religious discourse, I consider it theoretically significant to examine further the efficacy with which an international heritage discourse constructs and promotes a set of *beliefs in* heritage preservation while at the same time undermining other beliefs. Second, the rationalist and secularist model that dominates global heritage discourse needs to be understood in strict relation to its practical contexts and authorized disciplinary readings that construct these categories (Asad, 1993). The secular, in this discussion, is not indicative of an absence of "religion." It displaces one sensory and emotional repertoire by another (Jager, 2015). Examining the methodological approaches that have encouraged recon- ciliation with religious traditions, I will further argue that the apparent exclusion of religious thought in heritage preservation is neither unconditional nor com- prehensive. Global heritage and preservation discourse sometimes permits certain sacred traditions and rituals to take place and even thrive (cf. Bowman, 2012: 5).

Supported by the promising contribution of anthropological methods to heritage and preservation studies, two disciplinary turns encourage a reconsideration of the place of religiosity in the history and practices associ- ated with heritage discourse. One is the "material turn" in the humanities and social sciences that brings about a reappraisal and critical analysis of matter and materiality in the study of religion (Meyer and Houtman, 2012). This turn challenges the utility of categories of analysis such as "belief" and "religion" as largely Protestant legacies that should be reexamined within the interrelated conditions that shape religious practice. Accordingly, Section 2 reviews the ways in which these same legacies shaped the emergence of the Western canon for heritage discourse in alignment with long processes of secularization. This historical overview begins with the European wars of religion in the sixteenth century and proceeds through the emergence of global and institutional heritage discourse and its preservation ethos in the twentieth century. An eventual confrontation with "the spiritual" via recognition of alternative heritage practices that preexist or coexist with or resist Western heritage preservation gives rise to an academic and institutional redirection at the turn of the millennium when religion becomes a subject of dedicated institutional and disciplinary initiatives. What David Chidester has termed the "new materialism" in the study of religion redirects the focus of analysis to an examination of socially shared, authorized discourses that separate the material and the immaterial (Chidester, 2018). Likewise, the critical turn in heritage studies, concerned with the effects of a dominant global heritage discourse, constitutes the second disciplinary turn that provides a fertile ground for the study of the artifacts and effects of secularization on heritage discourse and practice.

In Section 3, I discuss the different zeitgeists through which spirituality and its exclusion have been confronted in the more recent history of the field through case studies that now form the backbone of a critical heritage tradition. The fact that universal heritage ideals continue to be summoned to mediate more recent preservation challenges in shifting religious contexts, such as the destruction of the Bamiyan Buddhas in Afghanistan or the conversion of the Hagia Sophia in Turkey into a functioning mosque, suggests that the anti-hegemonic heritage discourse that defines the critical turn fails to engage with its secularizing specters. The rematerialization of the study of religion (Meyer, Morgan, Paine, and Plate, 2010) and the spiritualization of the study of heritage invite an examination of heritage preservation practices in the context of different religious traditions but with particular emphasis on the frontiers at which competing semiotics coexist and are negotiated, and sometimes disrupted, by heritage preservation traditions (cf. Keane, 2018).

Section 4 offers a more equitable way forward. To begin, the section considers the recent practice of retrofitting heritage studies with a concern for religious values, which I argue to be inadequate for addressing the asymmetric encounter between religion and heritage traditions. I propose instead a critical and responsible reexamination of the disruptive nature of heritage and preservation discourses, the channels of expertise, and epistemological approaches that define much of the mission for critical heritage studies. In this concluding section, I propose a reflexive study of heritage and religion that supports a post-secular transformation in the discipline of heritage studies that is attentive to agency, ingenuity, and strategy.

For the purposes of this Element, I use the term "religion" pragmatically with a focus on establishing the contours of the debate rather than on proposing a definable category (de Vries, 2008). This means, for example, that I do not search for a distinction between the treatment of orthodox, institutional, and text-based religious practices and the beliefs and practices of "popular religions" that are particularly marginalized in global heritage preservation practices and discourses (Byrne, 2014). Likewise, throughout different sections of this discussion, I use the terms "religion" as an aggregate that encompasses "religion," "belief," "faith," and "sacrality." While such simplification may be sacrilegious in religious studies, these terms are used loosely by different authors and institutions across heritage preservation debates and policies, not least due to the claim that cultural heritage encompasses all dimensions. It therefore seems counterproductive to attempt to hierarchize such a heterogeneous terminology from the perspective of a field that has, as I argue throughout this Element, engaged very little with the subject matter of religion. In fact, I would argue that preserving the uses of terms like "religion," "belief," "faith," and "sacrality" in their discursive context reflects the fragmented way in which studies and policies for heritage preservation have approached and appropriated different aspects of religion.

For example, Britta Rudolff (2006, 2010) prefers to refer to a "heritage of faith" that stands for a representation of narratives inspired by faith. When examining global rapprochement efforts between heritage preservation and religion, Herb Stovel (2008) frames his arguments around a "sacred heritage," that is, a heritage whose principal source of meaning is faith. A contemporary UNESCO working group on religion defines heritage of religion sites as those that "possess components of religious significance and are recognized as holy cities by different communities" (UNESCO, 2010). At the same time, the "Filling the Gaps" initiative of the International Council on Monuments and Sites (ICOMOS) articulates "religious property" as "any form of property with religious or spiritual associations" (ICOMOS, 2004). Meanwhile, Britta Rudolff suggests that a heritage of faith is a "seemingly illegitimate category" after observing the ways in which religious buildings are grouped as historic buildings, while the intangible heritage of faith can simply be categorized as a dance or a festive event (2006: 77).

Conversely, distinct terms like "the secular," "secularization," and "secularism" have no significant footprint in the heritage literature. Benedict Anderson argued that the construction of imagined communities requires grounding on a secular and homogeneous time as well as on the constructed images that mediate that imagination (Anderson, 1983; de Vries, 2001). This Element considers that one such mediator, cultural heritage and its preservation, is produced by secularist ideologies that exclude religious experiences and authorities but not one that negates the existence of religious doctrine, institutions, or bodies. The exclusion of faith as epistemology does not erase sacrality in heritage value; rather, it subdues sacred narratives and authorities in heritage preservation discourses and practices. There is tension between the clear recognition of religious thought as a constituent of the places and traditions that form part of the assemblage of global heritage industries and the discomfort with religious thought in contemporary interpretations and uses of heritage. What is needed is an intentional and reflexive acknowledgment of these tensions to chart the future of critical studies of heritage.

2 Pressures of Secularism

The ways in which practices of heritage preservation are shaped by specific spiritual and religious discourses have been addressed partially in the literature of heritage studies. This literature also reflects on the evolution of secular cultural industries that closely shadow the advent of modernity (e.g. Smith, 2006; Harrison, 2013). While the story of the origins of a global heritage discourse is often located in mid-twentieth-century cosmopolitan engagements of UNESCO, the roots of a heritage preservation ideology extend back to the nineteenth century when the preservation of heritage became a formative instrument in nation-building projects across Europe.

Some scholars, however, recognize an earlier formative period that gives shape to heritage discourse in European territories: the secularization of religious spaces and performances that resulted from the European wars of religion from the sixteenth to the seventeenth centuries. For example, historicizing Western heritage thought, David Lowenthal summarizes the ways in which heritage value as an object of study was shaped by the rise of secularism starting in the Reformation in the sixteenth century. Here, he highlights the emergence of the idea of a posthumous human legacy that was disrupted in favor of secular and materialistic practices of remembrance. This shift saw ideological resistance to the Catholic Church manifested in a worldview that differentiated and compartmentalized distinct spheres of science and religion, a European secular rationalism that would eventually provide a foundation for the emergence of archaeological and heritage discourses (Byrne, 2014: 6). Denis Byrne calls the period that follows a "history of disenchantment." The dramatic changes brought about by the Protestant Reformation affected attitudes to places and objects by eradicating, marginalizing, and controlling the spiritual topography of Europe (Byrne, 2014: 40–43). Byrne describes how, while the doctrine of medieval Christianity had recognized, assimilated, and, to some degree, used pagan sacred landscapes and relics, the Reformation offered a doctrine and practice of worship disconnected from "spiritual" objects and places. The material culture of Christianity was rendered irrelevant by the internalization of worship, which, in turn, made embodied practices such as the pilgrimage and the spiritual glorification of the art and architecture of churches ancillary. The sixteenth-century Reformation also spelled neglect and destruction for the built landscape. The very fabric of Christianity was problematic for its embodiment of medieval Christian beliefs, and this resulted in processes of erasure such as the demolition of medieval abbeys in Britain (Aston, 1973).

The Catholic Counter-Reformation that followed brought about a spiritual revival in relationships and experiences of the landscape. During the European expansion of the sixteenth century, this ontology was productive for the assimilation of new indigenous religious landscapes, leading, for example, to the superimposition of Christianity on native sacred sites in the Americas. Later, through the European Baroque period, this type of transformation extended to sites that were not explicitly religious, including "islands, ruins, grottoes, androgynous bodies, and places of execution" (Eade, 2009: 241, quoted in Byrne, 2014: 46). Changes in spirituality and religious ideology, for example, manifested in Baroque overlays in Romanesque churches, whose interiors were dramatically reworked in ways that would constitute destruction by the standards of a modern preservation ideology (Schildgen, 2008: 15). The pressures of modern preservation standards on the dynamic liturgical needs of religion were not yet on the horizon. However, during this time, the field of archaeology emerged in line with the study of natural history as a mode of inquiry that centers on the systematic description of visually observable attributes (Schnapp, 1996: 205–212). A focus on new modes of documenting, ordering, and collecting produced a topography of secular "sites of significance" that would become heritage assemblages rooted in a rationalist modernity (Byrne, 2014: 45). The emergence of a "public sphere" in the seventeenth century and the rise of antiquarianism further enabled early processes of "heritagization" and turned such sites into historical monuments. Through these transformations, new forms of knowledge that derive from art historical and archaeological expertise and disciplinary languages emerged (Jokilehto, 2012). New disciplines were dominated by textual and two-dimensional pictorial representations that could be circulated and indexed. These shifts set the ground for the emergence of a field dedicated to the study and preservation of heritage significance that is centered in specific curatorial practices. The study of heritage was thus defined by a heavy reliance on measurement and precision, a dominant concern with the visual and tangible aspects of surfaces (Byrne, 2007), the establishment of listing and hierarchizing apparatuses (Rico, 2015; Harrison, 2016), and an emphasis on visual technologies of capture and representation (Shanks and Svabo, 2013; Hamilakis and Ifantidis, 2015; Brusius, 2016).

Through the eighteenth and nineteenth centuries, interest in recovery and preservation was on the rise. This was partly a reaction to the decay of cultural wealth in Europe (Mrijnissen, 2015: 278), an idea of aesthetics that separated abstract beauty from the particularities of faith, and also the replacement of the heroes and heroines of Christianity with a celebration of historic buildings in the service of the modern nation (Schildgen, 2008: 19). During this transition, the emergence of a formal heritage preservation tradition can be further territorialized and intimately weaved into localized narratives and politics of secularism that give shape to specific heritage preservation ontologies and technologies. Peter Pels describes a materialism during the Victorian era in the United Kingdom (1837–1901) that inherited a certain fear of matter from Protestantism. This materialism was most evident in different forms of iconoclasm (Pels, 2008). Intensified by a definition of the value of the human in "its distinctiveness from and superiority to the material world" (Keane, 2006: 314), Pels observes that a denial of the divinity of the soul and of the divine provenance of morality results in an alienation of objects from their context. This abstraction is reflected in early museum displays but also in the legitimization of the rule of experts in the social sciences (Pels, 2012). The Victorian period, with overlapping forces of industrialism, urbanization, and Darwinism, was not host to modern religious decline, but rather was marked by a preoccupation with the nature of religion and its function in the world that included a ritualist turn in anthropology (Lecourt, 2018). A good example of this concern is the way in which international exhibitions supported the emergence of a distinct field of religion for the Western intellectual landscape through curatorial practices and popular appeal (Burris, 2001). While earlier exhibitions lacked religious diversity (Cantor, 2011), a dedicated "World's Parliament of Religions," held in conjunction with Chicago's Columbian Exposition of 1893, constituted the first significant meeting of religious representatives from East and West (Kitagawa, 1993). Burris (2001) describes this moment as the culmination of a long history of curatorial practices that saw the alignment of religious and museum functions. It started with the housing and display of relics alongside other curiosities in churches that not only sanctified these spaces (Pomian, 1990) but also enabled the monopoly over certain areas of knowledge, first by the clergy and later by the (secular) humanists known as antiquarians.

In another key development in the emergence of heritage preservation discourse, a long and influential process of dechristianization that France traversed during the Revolution and the rise of the Republic (1789–1799) resulted in dramatic changes to the way in which the very materiality of religious practice was preserved in the built landscape. These transformations included the removal of plates, statues, and other fittings from places of worship and the destruction of crosses, bells, shrines, and other "external signs of worship," as well as the closure of churches (Tallett, 1991). A migration of the holy (or *transfert de sacralité*) that sees heritage-making as a secular sacralization of cultural goods during the nineteenth and twentieth centuries was intended to implement new intellectual rituals to create a form of civil spirituality (Isnart and Cerezales, 2020: 2–3). These changes also qualify the context for the emergence of the institution of the art museum in the late eighteenth and nineteenth centuries. In this context, Daniel Sherman (1989) describes the ways in which the revolutionary regime took on the burden of patrimonial preservation, utilizing secularized religious houses for the storage of confiscated property. Through this process of appropriation, many chapels characterized as "government buildings that were not already serving the public in some way" (Sherman 1989: 104) served the role of museum storage before purpose-built museum spaces were commissioned. The tensions between the declining value and the increasing utility of existing institutions defined curatorial attitudes and practices for the built landscape that would persist through the middle of the twentieth century (Atkin, 1991). Christian churches were also used in Russia for the establishment of new anti-religious museums by the Society of the Militant Godless during the 1920s and 1930s (Teryukova, 2014: 255–256). Within the privileged place that historical and artistic heritage was given in processes of nationalization, the institution of the museum should be seen as a key ideological weapon and tool for the growth of a scientific materialist ideology that increasingly redistributed authority over the past to emerging cultural institutions and experts.

Nascent heritage preservation agendas appropriated religious structures and functions to such an extent that fears of religious-led violence, social and political uprising, and territorial conflicts attached to the European wars of religion became embodied in the internationalization of preservation. That this was a Europe-wide phenomenon is evidenced by the attitudes of the ideologues of UNESCO toward religious traditions. By the middle of the twentieth century, the establishment of UNESCO as an international organization whose mandate was to build "peace in the minds of men" cautiously engaged with a fear of religion rooted in historical discourses omnipresent across Europe at the time. Following the 1905 Law of Separation of church and state, France struggled with the construction and use of and attitudes to commemorative monuments to the casualties of World War I (Sherman, 1999). Daniel Sherman gives a brief but clear glimpse into the way in which discourses of secularity are central to the politics of commemoration. He cites the example of debates about the careful inclusion and exclusion of religious emblems in public spaces and the exceptions allowed for buildings and monuments serving religious functions (e.g. cemeteries), as well as museums (Sherman, 1999: 236).

The specificity of France does not simply offer an examination of one of many milieus where the idea of heritage was drawn to do a particular work in the nation-building project across Europe. Rather, it constitutes a key examination of a *longue durée* politics of secularization across cultural institutions. More critically, it is fitting to recognize the influential role that France had in the eventual establishment of a global heritage preservation sensibility in the mid-twentieth century as a host of UNESCO and, more broadly, through its *mission civilizatrice*. The long processes of dechristianization that France saw during this period starting with the beginning of the Revolution in 1789 and the forms of expertise that emerged to replace Christian thought with a world view derived from scientific humanism are critical considerations in the emergence of a global and institutional heritage preservation discourse. The eventual rise of global heritage by UNESCO aligned with the governing secularist ideology of the time across Europe and helps explain UNESCO's hesitancy to engage in religious discourse.

2.1 Heritage Internationalization

The emergence of a global, institutionalized discourse for heritage is widely recognized to have occurred in the inter-war period in Europe, and this discourse was further developed in the historical and political context of the aftermath of the World War II. However, the story of the origins and growth of a universal model for heritage preservation that centers on this era obscures the religious ideology that is transmitted by key interlocutors prior to the official formative years. Melanie Halls' (2011) examination of the idea of "heritage protection" that circulated in the nineteenth century sets such antecedents of the international movement firmly within the context of empires and the Orientalism that gave rise to East–West discourses. Preservation campaigns during the period of 1870–1930 feature religion as a powerful factor in national and international preservation efforts. Many of the seminal texts associated with the rise of global curatorial practice were religious in nature, such as John Ruskin's *The Stones of Venice*. Hall (2011) points out that the Papal States were the first to receive heritage recognition following the return of heritage artifacts and the designation of Rome as a site museum in the Second Treaty of Paris (1815). The return of artifacts to a church-state asserted and demarcated the limits of secular authority (Hall, 2011: 10).

At the turn of the twentieth century, the appropriation of Hagia Sophia into Western consciousness as an icon of Christendom and Western civilization illustrates how a preservation discourse mobilized religious perceptions to serve political and ideological agendas. Erik Goldstein (2011) highlights the role of European experts and their religiosity in encouraging anti-Muslim sentiment articulated through concerns with the materiality and stewardship of the site. Swiss architect Gaspare Fossati, charged by the Sultan in 1846 with the restoration of the Hagia Sophia, made architectural conservation a religious issue by condemning "the negligence of the Moslem officials" (quoted in Goldstein, 2011: 48). This condemnation reached William Morris, one of the founders of the Society for the Protection of Ancient Buildings (SPAB) in the United Kingdom. Morris was active in anti-Turkish politics. From 1919 onward, the SPAB reported unfavorably on the state of conservation of the Hagia Sophia and determined that it was "at risk," thus mobilizing a public movement to have the building placed in Christian hands in alignment with Britain's interest in liberating Christian holy places (Goldstein, 2011: 55). Eventually, its designation as a museum and international monument in 1935 allowed for the discursive neutralization of its spiritual function for the global preservation community. Goldstein's examination illustrates the ease with which religious and political agendas inflected by imperialism are operationalized through global preservation discourse.

The official era of heritage internationalization and cooperation began in the inter-war period and was marked by the foundational work of the League of Nations' International Committee on Intellectual Cooperation (1925–1946). In 1931, they established the Standing Committee on Letters and Arts of the League of Nations. That same year, the committee organized the first International Congress of Architects and Technicians of Historic Monuments. The key output of this international congress, the Athens Charter for the Restoration of Historic Monuments (*Carta del Restauro*), set the tone for things to come by focusing on monumental sites and embracing a one-world concept of cultural heritage. Lowenthal argues that this concept gives birth to a discipline marked by Western languages, drawn by the hands of European experts. Non-European representatives from Tunisia, Mexico, and Peru did not join this conversation until 1964 (Lowenthal, 1998: 5). With such strong attachments to Western and European thought, these beginnings draw a narrow space for the eventual consideration of diverse religious traditions in heritage preservation agendas.

After pausing its operations during the World War II (1939–1945), the work of the standing committee fell under the umbrella of the newly established UNESCO and its culture sector. The delegation of the United Kingdom proposed that the headquarters of UNESCO should be established in Paris in recognition of "the effort made by France in the cultural sphere" and the "universality of the French spirit" (Valderrama, 1995: 24). Ironically, the inauguration of UNESCO was officially proclaimed in November 1945 at the headquarters of the Church of England, Church House, next to Westminster Abbey in London (Hoggart, 1978). The first director general of UNESCO, Julian Huxley, was a member of the Rationalist Press Association (RPA) whose members considered religion to be the main threat posed to society (Meskell, 2018: 2). His grandfather, Thomas Henry Huxley, had been such a strong proponent of the secularizing movement of the late nineteenth century that he had earned the title "The Pope of Agnosticism" (Pels, 2008). Peter Bowler points out that Julian Huxley, contrary to most members of the RPA, remained uncomfortable with the extreme rejection of all religious beliefs (Bowler, 2014: 317). Concordantly, Huxley wrote in his 1946 manifesto titled *UNESCO: Its Purpose and Philosophy* that the modern world has laid "undue emphasis on the intellect as against the emotions and on material as against spiritual satisfactions" (2010: 55) resulting in the neglect and distortion of the arts. In his statement, Huxley proposes that UNESCO's influence can ensure that art takes its place as an equal partner to science and technology in human affairs.

The voices that are invited to partake in the early initiatives of UNESCO reflect Huxley's vision. For example, the opening address for the Second General Conference of UNESCO in Mexico City was delivered by the French Catholic natural law philosopher, and later, monk, Jacques Maritain. Maritain had been invited to write the introduction to the volume *Human Rights: Comments and Interpretations* (UNESCO, 1949), the culmination of the controversial efforts by Huxley to contribute to the United Nation's 1948 Universal Declaration of Human Rights. In 1947, Huxley coordinated and launched the global questionnaire "The Grounds of an International Declaration of Human Rights" aimed at defining cross-cultural principles through a collation of voices around the globe, including contributions by Catholic scholars and theologians who "[took] issue with (its) overly humanist or liberal grounding" (Goodale, 2018: 38). The diversity of these voices was greatly exaggerated, with 45 percent of responses coming from the USA and the UK. Representations of the "non-Western" world came from a small group of responses that, Goodale argues, did not really present "arguments for how human rights are consistent with Hindu and Islamic traditions. Rather, in responding to the dictates of UNESCO/Phil/1/1947, they read as attempts to demonstrate how even a Hindu or Muslim can support a Western, liberal conception of the 'rights of man'" (2018: 35). Such a misrepresentation of diverse thought traditions around the world, exacerbated by the distortions of colonialism, lays a problematic grounding for the politics of spiritual inclusivity. The religiosity embedded in the foundational principles and doctrinal documents of the international era for heritage preservation is intertwined with the issues of misrepresentation and underrepresentation of non-Western and non-Christian traditions.

A review of UNESCO's founding documents suggests an institutional resistance to acknowledging religious values and spiritual forces as constituent parts of heritage value, reflecting unease by the leadership with the role of emotion in cultural decision-making strategies and, therefore, with the inclusion of religious belief, institutions, and leaders in the scope of its work. In practice, the religious sphere was kept ideologically at bay in UNESCO's principles and scope of work. Significantly, the preparatory commission charged with setting up a functioning UNESCO was confronted as early as 1945 by the delegation of Iraq, who pointed out the lack of representation from Arab-speaking countries despite the choice of five eligible delegations. Failure to have representation from the "views and hopes of the Moslem World" in the deliberations of the commission would, they argued, impede effective cooperation between the Middle Eastern states and the European and American nations represented in UNESCO. Concerned with the purely European outlook and a legacy that was predisposed to marginalize the needs, circumstances, and difficulties of non-European nations, the delegation of Egypt proposed the establishment of a permanent center of UNESCO in Cairo to act as a link between the seat of the Organization and the National Commissions of the countries represented in the Arab League but was unsuccessful. Lynn Meskell has described this disparity in the early phases of the organization as reflecting a "one-way flow . . . from the West to the rest" (Meskell, 2018: xvi) resulting in a mobilization of heritage that was unable to incorporate living aspects attached to rights of inclusion, access, use, and benefits, including religious benefits. The visibility of religion is therefore intertwined with the voices and forms of expertise that were invited to construct institutionalized global heritage preservation through technical assistance, capacity building, and, later, community consultation.

UNESCO's vision for the global preservation of heritage resources materialized in 1959 around a site rich with religious traditions: the Nubian temple complex of Abu Simbel threatened by the construction of the Aswan High Dam. UNESCO's efforts involved the relocation of a cluster of structures of Pharaonic Egypt that undoubtedly carry religious associations, destined to become one of the earliest inscriptions to the World Heritage List of UNESCO in 1979 under the name of "Nubian Monuments from Abu Simbel to Philae." This decades-long international safeguarding project set in place the collaborative discourse and diplomatic exchanges that normalized the idea of a heritage of religion disambiguated from the religious tradition that originated it. The process of heritagization that was set in motion in this archetypal safeguarding project favored historical and aesthetic values, not religious values, an emphasis that was maintained in practice and in doctrinal documents during the early decades of UNESCO's heritage work. As a site associated with a "dead" religious tradition, there was no documented voice of resistance countering the site's disassembly, relocation, and even export. Accordingly, the site's religious function was not considered to be compromised. The relocation of the living communities attached to Nubia, the "living" culture attached to this heritage assemblage, was rendered invisible (Mossallam, 2012; Meskell, 2018: 222). With this artificial separation, any cultural dimension of heritage value that communities could have contributed to these sites was eradicated. Some of the temples in Nubia were extracted and exported through international diplomatic and research transactions that emphasized the idea that their value was in no way related to their historic location or contemporary communities. The redistribution of these temples reflects a legacy of colonialism in the African continent: the Temple of Dendur was sent to the Metropolitan Museum of Art in New York, the USA; the Temple of Debod to the Parque del Oeste in Madrid, Spain; the Temple of Taffeh to the Rijksmuseum van Oudheden in Leiden, the Netherlands; and the Temple of Ellesyia to the Museo Egizio in Turin, Italy.

Perhaps it is not surprising that religion as a force involved in heritage-making was unaccounted for in the earlier texts that built momentum for the global era of heritage preservation. The binary opposition of the categories *natural* and *cultural* heritage on which the early operations of UNESCO and its advisory and affiliate organizations are built indicated a compartmentalization that would prove to be incompatible with the way in which history, the past, landscapes, culture, and identity were experienced by different people across the world. The establishment of UNESCO's classificatory system was formalized in the International Charter for the Conservation and Restoration of Monuments and Sites, known as the Venice Charter, drafted in 1964 by the Second International Congress of Architects and Technicians of Historic Monuments in Venice. It was then adopted as the gold standard of a new advisory body to UNESCO created at the same conference, the ICOMOS, in 1965. Considered to be the formative text of modern preservation ethos, the Venice Charter sets forth principles of conservation based on an idea of authenticity that resides in the historical and physical contexts of a site or building. It also reflects and justifies the organizational structure of UNESCO and its advisory bodies, whose effectiveness and authority lean on national and regional committees. While the text of the Venice Charter aligns with and reiterates a need for international principles to guide the work of heritage preservation worldwide, its preamble also states that "each country [should be] responsible for applying the plan within the framework of its own culture and traditions" (ICOMOS, 1965). In this way, the same invitation to recognize localized production of value would be used later to diversify ideas of heritage and preservation. Herein lies the most promising and vulnerable instrument for increasing global representation and support for a heritage of religion.

The pinnacle of international cooperation was reached through a different foundational document, the 1972 Convention Concerning the Protection of the World Cultural and Natural Heritage, often referred to as the World Heritage Convention. It made official two main concerns in the work of UNESCO: (1) the preservation of cultural sites and (2) the conservation of nature. Despite such a broad-ranging embrace of heritage value, the definitions in the text continue to exclude the spheres of religion (including ideas of "belief" and "the sacred"). For example, cultural heritage is defined in Article 1 of the World Heritage Convention as comprising "monuments" and "groups of buildings" that contain universal value "from the point of view of history, art or science" (UNESCO, 1972: Article 1), while universal value in "sites" is recognized "from the historical, aesthetic, ethnological or anthropological points of view." There is limited space in these restricted definitions for a consideration of religious objects, places, and practices, and for the articulation of values by religious authorities.

There are two instruments attached to the World Heritage Convention that display the efforts and challenges associated with the inclusion of religion in the cultural sector of UNESCO in dynamic and changing contexts: the Operational Guidelines for the Implementation of the World Heritage Convention (Operational Guidelines) (UNESCO, 2019) and the World Heritage List (List). The Operational Guidelines can be updated to reflect changes to what constitutes heritage value, significance, and forms of authority. Therefore, the mobilization of the concepts of "religion," "belief," and "sacred" over the decades reflects in these guidelines a certain difficulty with incorporating religious discourse in the work of the World Heritage Committee. Many of these revisions result from a confrontation between the principles laid out by the Venice Charter and the recognition of different heritage values in non-Western regions that are featured in ancillary documents. For example, in 1992, the World Heritage Convention recognized the category of cultural landscapes at its sixteenth session, defined in part as reflecting "techniques of sustainable land-use, considering the characteristics and limits of the natural environment they are established in, and a *specific spiritual relation to nature*" (UNESCO, 2019: 83, my emphasis). In a more recent revision, the idea of cultural landscapes allows for the inclusion of religion among the contributing forces of heritage value in different categories: designed landscapes associated *with religious or other monumental buildings and ensembles*; organically evolved landscapes resulting from an initial social, economic, administrative, *and/or religious imperative*; and associative cultural landscapes *justifiable by virtue of the powerful religious, artistic or cultural associations of the natural element rather than material cultural evidence* (UNESCO, 2019: 87).

The establishment and growth of the List in 1978 provided a steady stream of potential and actual conflicts that could be featured and examined in a structured arena in which different value systems had to be negotiated. The List has included sites associated with religious traditions since its earliest days; many successfully attached to the discourse and operational models of the World Heritage Convention under different typologies. By examining the heritage of faith during the period of 1978–2008, Britta Rudolff describes a complicated cartography of faith that relies on inappropriate terminology such as the use of the phrase "associated with" that downplays the authority and agency of religious narratives of faith (2010: 109). She further argues that ICOMOS evaluators charged with legitimizing faith-based narratives disparaged religious dimensions, preferring instead to bolster the material features of a site (Rudolff, 2006: 79). Resistance to the tenets of the World Heritage Convention, therefore, came not from within its geographical and ideological center in Europe, but rather from non-Western experiences of heritage preservation in the 1980s. For example, the Bangkok Charter of 1985 proclaimed and justified a local resistance to the restrictions imposed by the Venice Charter on the restoration of Buddhist monuments in Sukhothai (Byrne, 2004). In addition, through the 1990s, the credibility of the World Heritage Convention and the World Heritage Committee was shaken by the lack of representation featured on the List. This became the subject of scrutiny and research by UNESCO and its advisory bodies as well as through an emerging academic field of heritage studies.

By 1994, a deeper exploration of issues of representation in the growing List was underway, pressed by examinations of the Eurocentric roots of the Convention (Cleere, 2001), and the global applicability of universal values (Byrne, 1991). These interventions drew attention to an inadequate consideration of religious values in the scope of work of the World Heritage Committee, among other significant omissions. Expert meetings and thematic studies between 1994 and 1998 aimed to assess and redress the uneven representation that was noted in the growth of the list until that point. The *Global Strategy for a Representative, Balanced and Credible World Heritage List* (Global Strategy) of UNESCO was presented at the eighteenth session of the World Heritage Committee in Phuket, Thailand, in November 1994 (UNESCO, 1994). In the Gap Report that summarizes these findings, the absences in the List are quantified and qualified, to some extent, along *geographical* and *typological* biases

(ICOMOS, 2004). While the majority of sites on the List was predominantly comprised of historic and artistic resources in Europe, the Global Strategy concluded that the list also overrepresented historic towns and religious buildings, reflecting a chronological bias that favored historic periods at the expense of prehistory and the twentieth century and a social bias that supported "elitist" forms of architecture over vernacular forms. Although the list features religious traditions, the Global Strategy described an overrepresentation of Christianity over any other religious tradition. However, Britta Rudolff has questioned the way in which the presence of a heritage of religion was characterized in these reports, arguing that the analysis of representation such as the one that was carried out and disseminated by Sophia Labadi (2005: 90, 2007) ignored the ways in which a heritage of religion was mobilized throughout the corrective efforts: cathedrals – often French, but generally European – became a symbol of the phenomenon of imbalance and overrepresentation in many of these debates, "as well as a reference for literally all difficulties in the conception of outstanding universal value, colonial history, and cultural diversity in the World Heritage Committee" (Rudolff, 2010: 111). The heritage of Christianity was also identified as lacking support on the list. Rudolff and others (Rico 2008) have questioned the lack of critical examination of the typologies used for the quantitative analysis that sustains the conclusions of the Global Strategy. Nonetheless, in line with intellectual developments through the 1990s that precipitated a more critical engagement with heritage value, this reflexive moment in the work of the World Heritage Committee brought to light an inadequate consideration of *living* cultures in the sphere of work of the World Heritage Convention. As I discuss in Section 3, a separate and reactive engagement with heritage value focuses on the identification, incorporation, and management of non-monumental traditions, living expressions of human culture, and, more generally, categories and processes of meaning-making not previously considered by the World Heritage Convention and its advocates. Included and, I propose, driving, this rupture in the field is the question of religious traditions in the work of heritage and preservation.

2.2 Reparative Reconfigurations

The Global Strategy proposed to redress imbalances in the List through a set of coordinated initiatives, including thematic and comparative studies, expert meetings focused on underrepresented geographical regions, and other efforts that ensure the ratification of the World Heritage Convention across underrepresented regions (identified as the Pacific Islands, Eastern Europe, and African and Arab states). Accompanying this diversification, the pivotal Nara

Document on Authenticity of 1994 spurred a significant redirection in the scope of work of the World Heritage Convention (ICOMOS, 1994).

The Nara Conference on Authenticity in Relation to the World Heritage Convention reflected increasing awareness of "living heritage" that revolution-ized the way in which assessments of authenticity and integrity were carried out for World Heritage listings. As such, it marked a break away from the material-ist focus of the 1964 Venice Charter and sets the tone for the critical turn in heritage studies that gained momentum through the late 1980s. A key contribu-tion of the Nara document is the way it redescribes authenticity through a variety of previously ignored attributes, one of which is "spirit and feeling." The Operational Guidelines incorporated these principles to state that "attri-butes such as spirit and feeling do not lend themselves easily to practical applications of the conditions of authenticity, but nevertheless are important indicators of character and sense of place, for example, in communities main-taining tradition and cultural continuity" (UNESCO, 2019: 27). Such a statement exhibits an ingrained unease with religious and spiritual forms of authenticity. It proposes a separation between *recognizing* and *authorizing* a religious tradition in the construction of heritage value.

During 1995–1996, this unease became more apparent during the nomination and inscription process of the Hiroshima Peace Memorial (Genbaku Dome) to the List. Genbaku Dome was nominated by Japan as "a permanent witness to the terrible disaster that occurred when the atomic bomb was used as a weapon for the first time in the history of mankind . . . the only building in existence that can convey directly a physical image of the tragic situation after the bombing" (ICOMOS, 1996: 115). While the delegations of the United States of America and China resisted this nomination on political and ideological grounds, and issued warnings against the politicization of the List, it was the World Heritage Committee's reconsideration of the use of Criterion vi in the Japanese nomin-ation that endangered the integrity and global validity of the List. The twentieth session of the Committee in 1996 approved the Japanese inscription but announced the reduction of Criterion vi, to "be directly or intangibly associated with events or living traditions, with ideas, or with beliefs, with artistic and literary works of outstanding universal significance" (UNESCO, 2019: 25), so that it could only be used in exceptional circumstances (UNESCO, 1996). Superficially, the triumph of static materialist values preferred by the organiza-tion over the fluidity of intangible values encompassed by Criteria vi was expected, given the trajectory of the work of the 1972 Convention. However, this shift effectively enacted a politically driven reconfiguration for the List in two ways: (1) it revealed a strong secularist tradition that aligns with the dominant political block in the World Heritage Convention and (2) it restricted a category in ways in which it would also restrict the heritage of many non-Western nations on the World Heritage platform. Some critics have downplayed the effects of this restructuring. For example, it has been argued that a criterion used specifically to refer to "beliefs" raised the delicate question of putting a particular religion on the List, rather than the material culture of a religion (Bumbaru, 2008), while none of the World Heritage inscription criteria refers explicitly to expressions of faith (Rudolff, 2010: 100). Nonetheless, this untimely decision gave little weight to the significance of living heritage and expressions of belief, reducing the types of property that could be nominated to the List and undermining the efforts set out by the Global Strategy.

The twenty-first century brought with it a proliferation of charters and principles offering new definitions and terminologies for heritage that expand the potential presence and influence of religious traditions, discourses, and experts in the work of heritage preservation. A set of UNESCO Proclamations of Masterpieces of the Oral and Intangible Heritage of Humanity set out to raise awareness about intangible heritage (in 2001, 2003, and 2005) by listing the world's intangible cultural heritage (ICH). Relatedly, the UNESCO Convention for the Safeguarding of the Intangible Cultural Heritage was launched in 2003, putting emphasis on "practices, representations, expressions, knowledge, skills ..." (UNESCO, 2003a: Article 2). This definitional turn amplifies the principles of the 1989 UNESCO Recommendation on the Safeguarding of Traditional Culture and Folklore (UNESCO, 1989). It significantly broadened the conception of heritage through the recognition of the key role of "people, their learned process and knowledge, skills and creativity" (UNESCO, 2003a: Definitions) in the identification and safeguarding of cultural diversity. However, its promise for the support of religious traditions in heritage preservation may be larger than its actual impact.

While one can expect narratives underlying expressions of faith to be far more likely to be reflected in the recognition of intangible heritage, Rudolff notes a problematic deployment of terminology throughout these initiatives: almost every cultural expression listed in the Proclamations can be considered an expression of identity in the context of faith, yet "there is not a single reference to religion, faith, sacredness, or spirituality, in either the policy documents or the masterpiece program or the Intangible Heritage Convention" (2010: 115). Accordingly, Yujie Zhu discusses how the categories for ICH were used to culturalize religious practice in China: the Dongba religion listed as art and dance, Dixi of Guizhou as traditional drama, and the shamanistic ritual performance of the Budai people of Guangxi as dance (2020: 103). The practice of highlighting the cultural functions of religious traditions was also enforced by ICOMOS advisors to the List, who attributed sacred settlements and mountains to the category of "sites," rather than spiritual places, while all pilgrimage places were cataloged under the category "movement of people" (ICOMOS, 2004: 34–36). The colonial baggage that these institutional heritage categories reinforce comes into play through these arrangements. At the twenty-ninth committee session in Durban in 2005, the ambassador for India reflected that he is conditioned to bestow value over a cathedral with outstanding universal value over a site in his native India (UNESCO, 2005; Rudolff, 2010: 111). Rudolff also highlights specific reservations that state parties expressed over the possible inclusion of "religion" in the definition of intangible heritage. While some States considered the inclusion of religion in the World Heritage Convention a challenge to their constitutional standing in terms of the separation of religion and state, Japan objected on account of a view that "religion is an issue rooted within the minds of individuals, and hence does not appropriately lend itself to protection under this convention" (UNESCO, 2003b: 19). In addition, concerns were raised with the use of religion as an ideological tool (Rudolff, 2010: 117), a category of heritage value whose influence, she argues, is harder to limit than those of tangible heritage (cf. Jensen, 2000: 38).

The first decade of the millennium saw these agencies attempts to confront the unique challenges of operating on sacred places and the need to adopt standards and practices to this type of historic resource (Stovel, 2008) through a more intentional engagement at the intersections of heritage preservation and religion. A concern with religion was the center of various interrelated studies and initiatives throughout the 2000s. These included the forum in the conservation of Living Religious Heritage launched by the International Center for the Study of the Preservation and Restoration of Cultural Property (Stovel, Stanley-Price, and Killick, 2005), a 2005 resolution at the General Assembly of the ICOMOS calling for a thematic program that also defined the focus of the International Day for Monuments and Sites for 2008 as "Religious heritage and sacred places" (ICOMOS, 2008b), and resolution at the 2011 ICOMOS General Assembly reiterating a concern with the protection of sacred sites (ICOMOS, 2011: 20). A task force on the cultural and spiritual value of protected areas propelled a collaboration between UNESCO's Man and the Biosphere Programme and the International Union for Conservation of Nature (IUCN), which resulted in the 2008 UNESCO guidelines for the conservation and management of sacred natural sites (Wild and McLeod, 2008). Within the framework of the United Nations International Year for the Rapprochement of Cultures in 2010, UNESCO launched the Initiative on Heritage of Religious Interest, which included the Kyiv Statement on the Protection of Religious Properties within the Framework of the World Heritage Convention. UNESCO recognized that approximately 20 percent of the properties inscribed on the List have some sort of religious or spiritual connection and proposed in 2011 a thematic paper to provide general guidance regarding the management of cultural and natural heritage of religious interest (UNESCO, 2011). There is, throughout these coordinated initiatives, a sense of oversimplification of precisely how different faiths and the values that they espouse are reflected tangibly through material culture. These documents, for example, assume that the relationship between religious and heritage traditions is accessible to assessment by heritage experts, able to be made public, and translatable to a global audience. No mention is made of the different philosophical and material approaches that may be held by different religious traditions. Optimistic handling of a heritage of religion reflects the fact that these definitions are modelled from a selection of sites that have been indoctrinated into the scope and aims of the World Heritage Convention and have, therefore, already been made compliant with the ideals and forms of consumption promoted by global heritage discourse.

Furthermore, throughout these initiatives and documents, the voice of religion is recognized but not engaged with. Discursively and practically, these initiatives suggest that preservationists see themselves as having a function for society that is equal to the practice of faith, a claim that many believers would dispute. Additionally, preservation is proposed as having the power and responsibility to mediate religious dissonance (Stovel, 2008). In turn, religious communities are bestowed with the responsibility to "care" for themselves (i.e. their own heritage) in line with the principles of heritage preservation, an idea that suggests that heritage preservation advocates have control and authority over religious authorities and their agendas. The hierarchizing doctrine that puts preservation over religion is reinforced, for example, in a call for "balancing" the needs of faith and conservation on the same moral grounds. An intention to problematize changes in materiality, marked by a concern with the adaptation of sacred buildings over time, is disproportionally significant to the work of preservation. The way in which these objectives are articulated speaks to a key axiom in the conservationist mindset, one that presumes that physical change is a subject of concern for all parties involved in the use and appreciation of this type of historic resource. The Initiative on Heritage of Religious Interest invokes a legacy from UNESCO's Man and the Biosphere program that claims that "sacred sites ... are indeed the oldest protected areas of the planet" (UNESCO 2010). This claim puts religious and heritage practices along a shared path that glosses over the diverse ways in which religious contexts and living, dynamic practices of faith confront the agenda of heritage preservationists. What the documents attached to such a claim fail to consider is the possibility that the agenda of heritage preservation in a historic resource of religious value may not be co-constructed, but rather imposed. In this sense, the sphere of global and international heritage discourse has required the acquiescence of religious authorities and their communities into a preservationist mission without reciprocity. The result is a transformation of heritage of religious traditions into heritage of global secularizing traditions that excludes or trivializes religious forms of authority. In addition, religious sites have not always been protected and maintained in a way approved by preservationists, which has exacerbated the tendency to exclude key believer-stakeholders and resulted in the phenomenon that has been called "monumental vacuity" (Hertzfeld, 2006) – the erasure of social and cultural meaning by heritage practices themselves.

3 Legacies

While changes in religiosity have significant influence over cultural policies that have given shape to the idea of heritage and preservation in the preformative and formative phases of the discipline, the emergence of a global and institutional heritage discourse built on predominantly European processes of secularity actively sets itself apart from the religious thought that informed it. The intentional separation and even erasure of religious legacies in the growth of the global discourse for heritage and preservation constitutes a significant obstacle in the more recent reconsideration of the place of religious discourse in this field. These efforts, as discussed in Section 2, are dominated by the positionality and interests of the heritage and preservation field and its established discourses and practices. Therefore, I would argue that recent attempts at reconsidering the role of religious thought, communities, and practices are marked by an epistemic injustice (Fricker, 2007) that derives from the particular ways in which secularist discourse and practices are embedded in the idea and circulation of global heritage.

Throughout most of global heritage preservation history, religious value has been recognized and activated within the hierarchical structures and priorities of heritage preservationism. This can be traced through strategic and nondisruptive initiatives that translate religious thought into simplified and unidimensional engagements, rather than engage in equitable and potentially uncomfortable confrontations with the value systems, forms of authority, and expertise that sustain diverse religious practices. As a result of this unproductive encounter marked by hierarchization, global heritage discourse has proven to be particularly ineffective at normalizing religious thought and practice as well as managing the politics surrounding the preservation of religious heritage. By the

1990s, the relatively successful expansion of the global heritage discourse as it had been institutionalized in the heritage work of UNESCO raised new concerns. At a broad scale, these concerns can be defined by recognition of *alterity* in heritage value, its preservation, and study. In Section 2, I summarize some of the institutional actions responding to this newfound awareness. These efforts can be characterized as a proliferation of statements, initiatives, and doctrinal documents that aim to chart a rapprochement of heritage typologies and stakeholders that were once peripheral and incorporate them at or near the center of the global heritage discourse. In this section, I survey a different response that results from this awakening: the rise and growth of a critical heritage turn that promises to re-center the field of heritage and preservation on this recognition. The reconfigurations of forms of authority that define the critical heritage turn starting in the late 1980s offered an opportunity to normalize religious values in the work of heritage preservation in earnest. Therefore, this survey pays particular attention to highlighting the role of religious practices in the more recent history of heritage studies as a theme that defines the contours and objectives of this disciplinary turn.

The recognition that a heritage of religion functions in strict relation to specific practices and performances from the perspective of communities of believers (pilgrims, texts, and religious leaders) has been increasingly reflected in heritage preservation policy but in discreet contexts. For example, in 1979, Australia ICOMOS published the Australia ICOMOS Charter for Places of Cultural Significance, the Burra Charter, a document that brings local specificity to the Venice Charter and outlines the development of conservation philosophy in Australia. The Code on the Ethics of Co-existence in Conserving Significant Places, adopted in 1988 and contained in the 1999 issue of the Burra Charter, recognizes religious and spiritual beliefs among the definitions for values that construct significance for a cultural group (Australia ICOMOS, 1988: Article 1), while the latest update in 1999 extends the definition of cultural significance to include "spiritual value for past, present or future generations" (Australia ICOMOS, 1999: 2). Article 12 in the Charter, dedicated to "participation," states that "*Conservation, interpretation* and management of a *place* should provide for the participation of people ... who have social, spiritual or other cultural responsibilities for the place" (Australia ICOMOS, 1999: 5). Shifting ideas of responsibility, custodianship, and stewardship in relation to religious practice are reflected in the re-centering of heritage preservation discourse across various contexts. They are reflected in institutional and legal definitions (Tsivolas, 2019), funding regimes (Tanyieri-Erdemir, 2015), and a greater endorsement of nonacademic experts in heritage and preservation practice and policy overall. For example, the Cultural Heritage Committee of the Council of Europe adopted in 1998 a recommendation for the management of European cathedrals and other religious buildings in use, underscoring the fact that "religious communities have very different attitudes to their physical heritage" (Council of Europe, 2000: 347). At a global scale, and translated in documents that follow as well as in the work of heritage safeguarding organizations, the Nara Document of 1994 that was discussed in the previous section marks the first explicit mention of spiritual richness and belief systems, articulated as "spirits and feelings," that contribute to specific artistic, historic, social, and scientific dimensions of a cultural heritage. Thus, the sphere of the spiritual not only gained recognition as an essential aspect of human experiences but also invited a re-centering of the work of heritage preservation around new forms of knowledge that had not previously been considered. These new insights rested on archives, methodological approaches, and training traditions that fell outside of the scope of a preservation-oriented field of heritage studies. In addition, Nara asked experts to situate concepts, such as authenticity, within their own cultural spheres (Hafstein, 2018: 65). This process of cross-cultural discovery informed by cultural relativism invoked a concern with the way in which Eurocentric bias dominated the discipline. The positive reception of more anthropological concerns by institutions and experts failed to consider the way in which a history of secularism could impact the prospects of such a transformation.

3.1 After Nara

The critical turn in the field of heritage studies, therefore, is significantly marked by its intention to disrupt the hegemony of a "Western" discourse and its associated practices. It articulated its objectives through a two-pronged intervention. First, it recognized that post-Enlightenment views of material culture had defined a singular view of heritage value, one that was not representative of the diversity of material and immaterial engagements with culture and identity that were already observed by archaeologists and heritage managers around the world (Cleere, 2001). Second, the critical turn identified a poor fit between Eurocentric ways of thinking about and managing heritage value in non-Western social systems and values (Byrne, 1991) that some considered to be oppressed and endangered. This hegemonic discourse came to be defined by an amalgam of specific languages, instruments, and forms of expertise that empower the Western tradition of heritage preservation and are transmitted through colonial and imperialist agendas. In the critical heritage studies literature, it is often referred to simply as the authorized heritage discourse or AHD for short (Smith, 2006). While this turn has been discussed extensively with attention to the interdisciplinary histories that gave rise to it (Smith, 2006; Harrison, 2013), these accounts marginally consider the immense impact that an engagement with religious practices and discourses had in defining the objectives of this turn, whether deliberately or not, and the weight of secularist legacies that the turn was confronting. The apparent oversight may be due to the fact that any practices and discourses that fell outside of the hegemonic discourse were often articulated as "alternative" or "traditional" practices that prove the limits of the AHD.

In contrast, there are more specific concerns that are contained within the aims of a critical heritage turn and its support for alternative voices of authority (which I prefer to refer to as "non-disciplinary expert" to distinguish them from disciplinary experts) and alternative ways of knowing. Through these inquiries and a better awareness of secularist legacies embedded in both the AHD and anti-AHD ontologies and epistemologies, the centrality of religion can be made less opaque in the rise of the critical heritage turn, as can the limits of the turn itself. Many scholars and practitioners of heritage studies and preservation, especially those working outside of Anglo-American contexts, have referred to the AHD as simply a "Western" view, either ideologically or as a practical shortcut. However, the operation of the AHD is more complex than a simple breakdown of "East" versus "West" that characterized earlier conversations that were aimed at resurfacing ontological and epistemological distinctions across territories (e.g. Akagawa, 2015). In discussions of representation of religious traditions, for example, blanket engagements with Christianity that are mapped over simplified cartographies erase the complexity and diversity of Christian experiences (Ugolnik, 2016). Different modes of engagement with materiality and preservation, such as Orthodox Christian practices in Russia and Ethiopia that are similarly endangered by the AHD (Antohin, 2019), can be excluded from anti-AHD debates for a perceived alignment with an already overrepresented European category. The same is true for other religious traditions and regions.

The early phases of an investment into the recovery of pre-hegemonic, anti-hegemonic, or alternative views and uses of heritage emerged through the study of heritage practices across Asia, featuring spiritual and religious discourses at its core. Reporting from China, Wei and Aass spoke in support for the consideration of an "Eastern" emphasis on the *genius loci* (spirit of place) that differed from what they called a "Western" emphasis on objective reality. They used this contrast to propose specific approaches to heritage preservation beyond the Western paradigm (Wei and Aass, 1989). Soon after, Denis Byrne (1995) questioned the consequences of deploying modern global preservation practices and standards in his examination of the living religious temple of Ayutthaya Wat in Thailand. Observing that the spiritual and social values of Buddhist stuppa rely on their ability to be enlarged over time by encasing the older fabric in a new shell, Byrne argued that the privileging of "original" fabric in conservation practice prevents the addition of new material and, therefore, disrupts religious practice and value (Byrne, 1995). Advocating for the significance of decay in processes of value-making for Buddhism, Anna Karlström's (2005) close examination of Buddhist heritage sites in Laos demonstrates that an embrace of impermanence challenges the relevance and utility of the idea of integrity that is central to classical approaches to heritage preservation. Meanwhile, in Japan, traditional preservation practices surrounding Ise Shrine, extensively reconstructed every twenty years following the *Shikinen sengu* ritual, reinforce the legitimate authority of ritual practices over that of global and institutional standards (Adams 1998) .

Early case studies like these are joined by a common thread that defines the inclusion of sites of active religious practice into heritage assemblages. The value of authenticity, long used as a benchmark for legitimizing heritage significance, could no longer be expected to reside in a material antiquity defined by experts. This turning point constitutes the backbone of a critical study of heritage that puts the authority of religious practice on par or above that of heritage preservation practice. In doing so, it redescribes many of the keystones that had been used to carry out an effective universalization of a global heritage preservation tradition: "authenticity," "integrity," and even the art historical periodicity that helped locate a site in the patrimonial map. While it is clear that a broadly conceptualized Asian territory provided a fertile ground for exploring the question of alterity in heritage preservation, it is not synonymous with this turn. Elsewhere, Charlotte Joy's (2012) ethnographic study of the management of historic mosques of Djenné in Mali highlights the unique social practices that construct a meaningful authenticity against the grain of UNESCO's standards, distinguishing between a view from the outside informed by World Heritage Values and a view from the inside that is informed by social and spiritual practices of caretaking. Neither is the critical turn relegated thematically to the preservation of non-Judeo-Christian religious heritage. In Canada, Hilary Kaell revisits and expands the ethnological work of Jean Simard, who documented the practices of care for *croix de chemin* across rural Quebec, noting the way in which caretakers' practices of replacement, additions, and reconstructions of these wayside crosses localize ideas of continuity in direct opposition to the material coherence championed by heritage expertise (2019: 129–130).

The greatest contribution of the critical turn in heritage studies is not its resistance to the global relevance and authority of materiality as it is embedded in the Venice Charter and transmitted through apparatuses such as the List. Rather, its strength lies in the way it challenged forms of inquiry and rules of experts who promote an unequivocal universal experience and uncritical de-hierarchization of access to places of heritage significance. In this sense, the critical turn constitutes a reflexive turn. The studies mentioned above propose a closer examination of the ways in which preservation constitutes an *active* process of materialization (Buchli, 2002: 14–15), one that disrupts the materiality and ecosystem of values of places and practices alike and not simply a field whose only effect is the documentation and improvement of the conditions of this value. The recognition of the powerful epistemic forces that are deployed by the field of heritage preservation and a consideration of the competing value systems that are contained in the religious traditions that encounter it are compelling reasons to revisit preservation practices *as ritual practices* that enter into competition with other belief systems.

In practical terms, the coexistence of these two ontological realities has proven to be challenging. Heritage discourse, as I have discussed in previous sections, is largely defined by modern secular rationalism. Because of this, the field of preservation and its experts are encouraged to approach temples, for instance, as exclusively human artifacts rather than as phenomena that arise from an interpenetration of divine and human agency (Byrne, 2014), artifacts sustained by the modern Cartesian view that matter is inert and passive (Olsen, 2010). The disciplinary bias toward a positivist ontology has been integral to preservation thinking since the earliest conservation primers (cf. Ruskin, 1890; Riegl, 1982 ; Brandi, 2005). This bias is central to the canon of the discipline which encourages a direct correlation between the visual perception of conservators and their understanding of the object or place (Caple, 2000: 2). Its persistence in contemporary heritage management has implications for the incompatibility between the two ontologies that reside in heritage preservation and religious traditions. For example, in the Cambodian site of Angkor Wat, a "living" site that remains actively sacred despite having gained World Heritage status, Keiko Miura (2005) documents the effects of imposing a mixed-use management approach informed by modern preservation debates. This approach claims to reconcile the role of the heritage site as a religious site with the role of the living temple as a heritage site. The result is a documentation of a continuous exclusion of intangible "living" factors in decision-making at Angkor, particularly motivated by the commodifying forces of tourism (Miura, 2007). Also, the management strategy was set in place without any consideration of the way in which conservation decisions enforce the colonial politics of secularism. In a monumental site that boasts periods of coexistence and conflict through historical and religious transformations, conservator Simon Warrack

(2011) highlights the way in which colonial authorities at Angkor denied the monastic community the right to ownership of the site at the beginning of the twentieth century. Henceforth, conservation decisions were informed by a diminished and undermined religious and spiritual stewardship. Consequently, when Angkor Archaeological Park was nominated and inscribed to the UNESCO World Heritage List in 1992, authorities articulated its heritage tourism and ritual practices (and possibilities) in apparent harmony.

The historical subjugation of forms of authority that would ensure the performance and preservation of the sacredness of a site that has a role in religious traditions, therefore, contributes to its desacralization unless the field of heritage and preservation examines its own legacies and relationships to past politics and practices. Moreover, the discourses and economic pressures of a tourism industry often encase global heritage value and force two distinct uses of a site into a forced shared ontology, one that aspires to remain multivocal and inclusive in its interpretations and uses, despite a preferential alignment with global heritage over local sacrality. In practice, this disparity manifests eventually. The World Heritage Site of Uluru in Australia has been the subject of irreconcilable and contradictory interests: the visitation practices allowed and encouraged by a tourism industry attached to World Heritage designation are confronted by an Aboriginal sacred tradition that forbids the same visitation practices (Foxlee, 2009). Also, in the Kingdom of Saudi Arabia, the site of Madā'in Sāliḥ has gained World Heritage status, but visitation can be restricted to a broader public due to its specific spiritual role (Alrawaibah, 2014). The intersection of global heritage and tourism agendas is precisely what prevents the holiest historic site in Islam, Mecca, from having the ability to become a global heritage site (Rico, 2020). Some scholars examining religious heritage and tourism have argued in support of self-designated "pilgrim" identities that can claim the same rights of access to sacred sites as indigenous believers (Di Giovine and Choe, 2019). In addition, these debates propose that tourism is a catalyst for coexistence in this type of mixed-use sites (Di Giovine and Garcia-Fuentes, 2016), rather than a potentially disruptive or oppressive force. These arguments further the aims of a hegemonic and secularizing discourse that downplays the centrality of belief and its practice by appearing to credit economic forces attached to the tourism industry with a successful ontological blurring of secular and spiritual values and uses. With much of the concern placed on structural affinities and historical confluences, what remains poorly addressed in this type of debate is the uneven levels of privilege and agency that nonbeliever and believer pilgrims can possess to start with. Believer communities in sites that gain notoriety through models such as the List designation are already relinquishing much of the intimacy that is associated with the use of these places. Michael Strausberg suggests that the homogeneous tone of these debates may be due to the dominance of tourism scholars -not scholars of religion- in the sub-field that examines heritage, religion, and tourism (see an overview in Strausberg, 2011: 8–11). What they seem to be lacking is an engagement with the politics of indigeneity, especially as articulated through disciplines such as Indigenous studies, which prioritize discourses of Indigenous sovereignty that are often in friction with state regimes.

Seasoned debates in the field of archaeology provide a foundation for under-standing the politics of use and access in a heritage of religion, buttressing support for alternative and marginalized voices that are instrumental to the spiritual and social integrity of this type of resource. A concern with contem-porary sacrality became evident in the 1990 World Archaeological Congress (WAC) meeting in Barquisimeto, Venezuela, where a "Sacred sites/sacred places and 'sites of significance'" session motivated the adoption of a special resolution by the WAC Plenary Session and Council. WAC henceforth acknow-ledged "that the identification and conservation of sacred sites are of major concern to all the peoples of the world" and signaled an intention to further investigate and formalize an international accord on sacred sites, sacred places, sacred spaces, and sites of significance (Ucko, 1994: xiv). These earlier conver-sations drew from a precedent in Australian archaeology where, as early as 1972, a recognition of Aboriginal sacred sites brought up a concern with sacrality and secrecy that affects any efforts at documenting and collecting archaeological data. By 1977, the Australian Institute of Aboriginal Studies officially dictated that recording of sites of significance to Aboriginal people would be carried out only with the approval of Aboriginal custodians. In 1978, they established a recording policy for sites of significance through set methods of conservation and physical protection of sites that revolved around Aboriginal involvement, standards, and priorities (Ucko, 1979: 14). The recognition of a definition of sacrality that extended beyond disciplinary control and disciplin-ary orders of classification resulted in a commitment for cooperative relation-ships that accept the legitimacy of traditional indigenous ways of knowing (Hubert, 1994: 11), as well as forms of documentation that re-center indigenous knowledge and even sovereignty (e.g. Byrne and Nugent, 2004).

In the adjacent field of museum studies, actions and reactions toward sacred value have been mixed. The examination of sacrality in relation to indigenous stewardship and rights of ownership of objects in museum collec-tions has been extensively represented, in both "Western" (Clavir, 1996, 2002) and "non-Western" contexts (Kreps, 2003, 2005, 2006). The specific treatment of objects of religious significance, their preservation and display, and the relationship to their legitimate stewards, past, present, and future is as diverse as there are institutional and national trajectories (Sullivan, 2015). At one end of the spectrum, some scholars have suggested that a sacred object of art in a museum vitrine is essentially a different object from the one that is displayed in a temple altar, not simply the same object in different locales (Lachman, 2014: 375). This dichotomous proposition conveniently dissociates the transformation of these objects from the context and power structures that initiate and officialize the translocation and translation of sacred objects into museum collections. It is also often untenable: in one of the early articles that specifically address Muslim-appropriate conservation and handling of Qur'anic text, Zekrgoo and Barkeshli (2005) explain in no uncertain terms that the sacredness of the text does not cease to exist in the setting of the museum or conservation lab. At the other end of the debate and more in line with current de-colonial agendas, engagements with sacred objects in museums are accompanied by a recognition of different publics (e.g. a religious stakeholder vs. a scientific or academic stakeholder), and different forms of expertise and authority (e.g. a religious authority vs. a curator) involved in the acts of collecting and exhibiting these objects. Recognizing these distinctions, and the different ontologies that they espouse, dictates that the secular versus sacred identities and use-values (or social roles) of these objects often cannot coexist without significant conflict (cf. Arthur, 2000; Paine, 2013). However, as I argue throughout this Element, the nature of this conflict is not over the sites or objects themselves, but rather over the relative authority of voices and forms of expertise that make, unmake, mobilize, or paralyze sites and objects and their local communities.

3.2 Disrupting Conflict

The turn of the millennium not only marked a growing interest in the spheres of religion for the study and management of heritage resources but also was defined as, and is intimately tied with, two types of disruption to the dominant idea of heritage value and its management. The first disruption is a recognition of the ways in which sites of religious significance undermine calls for a universal heritage value and, by association, the validity of a global heritage discourse. The preceding paragraphs provide key examples of this tension. The other, less explored, disruption is an examination of the ways in which heritage expertise, through discourse and practice, is itself responsible for creating or exacerbating existing and potential tensions in sites of religious significance. In addition to marking one of the pivotal issues in the critical heritage turn, these disruptions are also significant for the way in which they invite a redescription of the field's conceptualization of conflict and, more critically, its constituent role in a conflict that revolves around a heritage of religion. The preceding case studies also provide context for the myriad conditions under which this is plausible.

Naturally, being the cause of destruction or devaluation of heritage significance runs counter to the core objectives of preservation. Therefore, heritage experts and institutions have actively shifted the narrative of conflict to call attention to that which occurs independently of the actions of heritage experts and institutions themselves. In focusing on their role as monitors rather than as agents in a conflict of values, they divest themselves of any responsibility that the field may have in contributing to the conflict itself. In reality, the relatively brief history of global heritage preservation is marked by instances of irreconcilable conflict and failed attempts at mediation surrounding sites of religious significance that serve to underscore the political nature of decision-making in heritage preservation. To be more specific, there are three iconic case studies which are often core to any syllabus that examines the politics of heritage.

First, the intentional destruction of the Bamiyan Buddhas in Afghanistan in 2001 by Taliban forces mobilized a discourse of religious-led iconoclasm that remains a prevalent theme in heritage studies (Meskell, 2002; Stein, 2018). This conflict set the tone for discussions on the difficulty of reconciling local-religious with global-heritage concerns. More significantly, it underscored the way in which heritage resources are used as a platform for religious and political agendas that are interconnected in complex ways (Flood, 2002; Elias, 2007; Rico and Lababidi, 2017). Following the failures of an international community of heritage experts to renegotiate the destruction of the Buddhas through the mobilization of a universal heritage value and expertise (and, some would argue, provoked by it), the destruction of the site was nonetheless assimilated into a global heritage assemblage through its inscription into the List in 2003 and re-ascribed as the "Cultural Landscape and Archaeological Remains of the Bamiyan Valley." The second example dates to one of the earliest global debates surrounding the politics of heritage, which has resurfaced more recently. In late 2019, the Supreme Court in India ruled in favor of the construction of a Hindu temple in Ayodhya at the site where the Babri Masjid mosque had been violently demolished in 1992. This conflict occurred at the threshold of the 1994 WAC in New Delhi, India and mobilized archaeological data strategically (Abraham, 2005). Babri/Ayodhya has remained at the center of a decades-long discussion about conflicting heritage values and the politics of heritage preservation in the context of religious tensions (Shaw, 2002; Silverman and Ruggles, 2007). Finally, in 2020, Turkish President Recep Tayyip Erdogan transferred control of the site of Byzantine monument Hagia Sophia to the Religious Affairs

Directorate by issuing a decree to open the site for Muslim prayer. This decision ended the eighty-year history of Hagia Sophia as a secular museum and it challenged the World Heritage Status awarded by UNESCO in 1985 when it was inscribed on the List as part of the "Historic Areas of Istanbul." Contrary to Ayodhya, Hagia Sophia has long been circulated in heritage discourse as a symbol of harmony and coexistence of multiple values as well as a symbol of the enduring significance of the universal value with which it was bestowed. The change of function and status is now seen by experts as a betrayal of these values, ignoring decades-old negotiations that resulted in its denomination as a museum in the first place (Goldstein, 2011). The common denominator in these heavily circulated case studies is the mythologized role for heritage expertise as a neutral observer and mediator that acts in the best interest of a belief in a universal value. Not only is this role imagined to have the ability to transcends conflict, but it is also a role unburdened by religiosity and by its own political engagements with secularism or sectarianism.

Taking an interest in conflict is one of the most defining legacies of the particular historical trajectory of heritage and preservation studies through its overarching concern with destruction and, in the case of religious-led conflicts, the mobilization of iconoclasm. Examining the history of the latter, Brenda Schildgen calls this concern part of the "symbolic capital" on which preservation practices rely. It derives from the outbreak of destruction that followed the French Revolution which made preservation "progressive" and destruction "retrograde" in European heritage (2008: 14–15). Later, the widespread destruction across the built landscape of Europe during the World War II provided a familiar staging ground for the emergence of global heritage concerns bound by the oppositional ideology that puts destruction at odds with preservation. What is addressed more sparsely in the history of heritage preservation thought thereafter is the ways in which preservation practices themselves are iconoclastic (cf. Rico, 2016). Therefore, the centrality of conflict in approaches to heritage of religion should not only be seen as the compounded effect of observed cases of intercommunal violence such as the highly circulated conflicts of Bamiyan, Ayodhya, Hagia Sophia, and so on. Conflict is also an instrumental raison d'être that defines the contours and approaches of the discipline.

While, occasionally, heritage debates do highlight coexistence and practices of care that thrive despite religious dissonance (e.g. Saifi and Yüceer, 2013), the strength of the dominant expectation for conflict calls attention to Glenn Bowman's advice to consider the way in which "the social fields encompassing the sacred spaces constitute those places, that is, relate to, and impact upon, the rituals which take place within them" (Bowman, 2012: 5). Related debates in anthropology propose a healthy dose of reflexivity and provide an additional point of reference for understanding the weight of anticipation of these tensions for the practice and discourse of heritage preservation. Bowman (2012) argues that much of the perception that sacred places hold inherently irreconcilable tensions derives from Bernard Lewis' idea of a "clash" between Islam and the West (Lewis, 1990) and the proposition that sacred sites are inherently indivisible due to the identities that they contain (Hassner, 2009). Rejecting these terms, Bowman instead proposes a consideration of identity as an emergent, situational, and ofttimes contingent property, examined through processes such as social interactions, ritual performances, and historical transformations. A significant body of work in anthropology provides supporting evidence of sharing in sacred places. For example, Anna Bigelow's (2010) ethnographic study of the town of Malerkotla in India, where worshipping Muslims, Sikhs, and Hindus harmoniously share stewardship of a Sufi saint's tomb shrine in an otherwise politically volatile region, offers a counter-narrative for the dominant perception of militant and intolerant religious stakeholders that have been more frequently featured in heritage studies. An extremely important aspect of Bowman's work, demonstrated in Bigelow's ethnographic accounts, is the commitment to document a sophisticated "choreography" of intercommunal relations around holy places (Bowman, 2012: 3; Barkan and Barkey, 2015). He also observes that the harmony that is imposed on a site through monolithic authorities in order to exclude differences and govern symbologies and rituals can result in greater tensions. Transporting this warning to the study of heritage demands a consideration of the degree of influence that a monolithic authority, in the shape of international heritage experts, organizations, and policy documents, may have on exacerbating conflict itself by imposing inflexible and indivisible categories of analysis.

Global heritage discourse and the methodologies that currently serve it have the ability to alter the conditions of coexistence and interrupt the possibility of "peaceful sharing" through practices of hierarchization of value and authority that are core to the articulation of heritage significance and value in global terms. Religious studies scholar Aike Rots (2019) summarizes the specific ways in which sites of religious significance are incorporated into the more rigid discourse of World Heritage and the serious consequences that this transformation has for worshipping practices. These consequences are diverse due to the different contexts in which they operate but fall into recurrent patterns (Rots, 2019: 155–156). First, he argues that such a shift of status de-privatizes religious sites and practices by enabling or strengthening control of secular authorities over them. In addition, Rots argues, acquiring a status such as World Heritage secularizes sites by diminishing the agency of private religious or other belief systems and attaching them instead to narratives such as the origins of the nation, collective identity, and so on. These explicit reclassifications serve the strategic purpose to establish government control over ritual practices. In his study of popular religion and heritage practices, Denis Byrne makes specific reference to the way in which secularist heritage preservation discourses and practices not only disregarded belief systems but were, in fact, used to intentionally target belief systems by governments, religious hierarchies, and reform-minded elites as a part of anti-superstition campaigns (Byrne, 2014: 1). Heritage discourse, in this sense, partakes in a form of destruction that is not necessarily visible through physical erasure (although it can eventually lead to it). Rather, this form of destruction entails a discursive transformation that reduces the religiosity of sites and places through secularization. Finally, Rots' (2019) analysis considers the rise in tourist visitation that is associated with World Heritage designation as a powerful force of transformation that leads to the re-ascription of sites as secular public property in the public imagination or even in legal terms. The concern with the rigid categories that are imposed on sites of religious significance, in this case, is not that devotional elements or religious actors disappear but that religious actors have to compromise and negotiate the demands of secular authorities, NGOs, and entrepreneurs resulting in what Rots calls "discursive secularization" (2019: 160–161).

The specific secularizing legacies that underpin both a global *and* a critical heritage discourse mean that "we cannot just add a living and popular religious heritage discourse to the institutionalized heritage discourse," as Anna Karlström argues (2013: 396). Beyond any conciliatory mechanisms that global heritage discourse may be claimed to have, by specific actors, it could be said that all heritage preservation practices remain rooted and attached to ideologies that center on objectification, rationalism, and secularism, making heritage preservation inherently ill-fitted to manage its own conflict with religious practices. The work and, to some extent, the scholarship in heritage preservation continue to show a lack of awareness of the ways in which it perpetuates secularist legacies, making heritage preservation a constituent part of conflicting authorities when it is involved in religious-led tensions. In other words, the intervention of a critical heritage tradition has demonstrated that institutional heritage preservation discourses and methodologies are ill-fitted vehicles for the examination of, and support for, alterity in general, as demonstrated in the marginalization of religion in the work of global heritage in particular. The promise of a critical turn is also unfulfilled. Despite significant reconfigurations, efforts at closing the gap between a materialist and a spiritual preservation philosophy have not challenged substantially the marginalization of living, spiritual traditions (Byrne, 2004: 19). In this sense, the path forward for a critical turn in the study and management of heritage has not been accompanied by an epistemic revolution and, instead, falls back on the same methodological principles that sustain the same global or institutional discourse that it seeks to confront. *Recognizing* the existence of a religious stakeholder and *empowering* a religious stakeholder to contribute or even take the lead in heritage preservation and management are different commitments.

4 The Critical (Re)turn

Since the 1970s, the waning of a Western humanist tradition is confronted by the material turn in archaeology, a widespread interest in the agency of objects, a symmetrical model of human–object relations, as well as a concern with embodied experience that falls under "affectivity" (Byrne, 2019). Byrne proposes that serious consideration of the supernatural as an orientation, a post-secular heritage practice, is most likely to come from within the field of critical heritage studies (Byrne, 2019: 9). Therefore, while the material turn in the study of religion is committed to taking seriously the material dimensions of religion and their role in the making of religious identity (Meyer, 2008), the critical turn in heritage studies must, in turn, engage with its subject of study beyond materiality.

The challenge in critical heritage studies is to resolve its own epistemic bias, that is, the way in which the production of knowledge in the discipline is bound by the contours of the very same hegemonic discourse that it is trying to resist. The commitment, then, is to reconsider and bring to the foreground the processes of creation of the empty, unexplored spaces beyond the dominant discourse in the work of heritage and preservation. Sociologist Eviatar Zeruvabel (2018) calls this type of epistemic territory the "unmarked," as opposed to the "marked." Through this distinction, he lays out a contrast between what is explicitly accentuated and that which is unarticulated – or *taken for granted* (Zeruvabel, 2018). In this way, the dominant and the alternative heritage discourses are often defined in contrast with each other. More specifically, the anti-AHD discourse and practice are largely defined by that which is not the AHD. Recognizing this relationship has important implications for the growth of the critical study of cultural heritage, as normality and abnormality are intentionally established by a hegemonic authority in order to sustain itself. However, at this juncture, both discourses, however opposed, are synchronized in their neglect to engage with secularist legacies integrated into the history and practice of heritage preservation and study. This proposes a reexamination of what exactly is left unarticulated in the work of heritage and preservation. The study of the invisible or unmarked is "methodologically elusive," as Zeruvabel argues; "acts of omission, after all, are much harder to notice than acts of commission" (2018: 9). Therefore, the epistemic challenge in a critical heritage turn is not resolved by simply applying the same forms of inquiry that have worked for a dominant heritage discourse to examine its counter-archive, as the field has mostly been doing. These tools are intimately attached to the hegemonic discourse itself. In Section 3, I argued that identifying and labeling religious practice as a type of alterity in the critical turn in heritage studies has only been part of the task. While these debates contributed to reshaping the contours of the discipline, they have not made progress with rethinking its content or rethinking ways of thinking about its content.

The practice of heritage preservation, therefore, has to tackle two extraordinary obstacles in this reckoning. One is the fact that a concern with religion that enters heritage preservation through the window of intangible heritage charts a problematic scenario: religious practices and their communities have clear tangible and spatial dimensions and cannot be synthesized as an intangible experience and reality. The second epistemological challenge is the allochronic and nonsequential way in which religious value is used in assessments of significance. In this timeline, religious traditions create the material culture on which heritage significance is assessed (through values like aesthetic, historic, social, etc.) and are also credited with ensuring its continuity through use. However, processes of heritagization and heritage governance that follows regard these places as containing intrinsic value instead, one that may stand independently from its religious purpose. This way, religious use is seen as an exogenous force that needs to be managed, since it can affect peaceful coexistence with heritage use. In this view, religion "enters" the debate in order to disrupt it, with little to no acknowledgment of the fact that a religious tradition is a fundamental force that created the possibility of a heritage in the first place. In considering this paradox, it seems that identifying something like a heritage of religion (or similar designations) is a terminology that anticipates the depreciation of religious claims. This practice of putting religious traditions to the service of heritage claims is precisely the structural problem that Anna Karlström (2013) condemns.

This Element revisits the intellectual and practical history of heritage preservation in its attempts to dissociate itself from, and then reengage with, religious traditions. It traces the trajectory of a field defined by a Eurocentric monolithic discourse with global aspirations that becomes fragmented into a series of practices and debates that attempt to diversify, recognize, and resist the hegemony of Eurocentric universal values. The identification of alternative ontologies continues to be epistemologically isolated from the study and management of cultural heritage. This separation and exclusion can no longer be explained by the relative invisibility of these practices, especially now that critical heritage scholarship has revealed the high frequency with which dominant heritage discourses overlay, sideline, or transform a pre- or coexisting practice of preservation and transmission of heritage value. The exclusion, instead, is better explained by the relative inaccessibility of the knowledge that comprises alternative heritage value, a knowledge that is obscured through the modes of inquiry that are predominantly practiced in the study of heritage. This under-representation can be attributed to the force with which the idea of alterity defined a non-AHD heritage debate. Not only is the idea of alterity able to erase differences among nonconforming heritage preservation traditions, but it is also a way of maintaining a heritage of religion distant from the core engagements of the discipline. Differentiating "sacred" or "religious" value from other values encourages other practices of valuation to be defined as secular. Through designations of alterity, the canon in heritage studies is allowed to remain, for the most part, coherent and aligned with the dominant heritage discourse. In this concluding section, I propose to shift the study of heritage and religion beyond an ontological concern to an epistemological reality.

4.1 Post-Secular Heritage Studies

The call for post-secularizing the study and management of heritage goes beyond recognition of the centrality of materiality and scientism that dominates heritage discourses and practices. It also goes beyond identifying and documenting the marginalia that lie outside of the boundaries, frontiers, borders, and edges that are generated by the operation of a global heritage preservation discourse (Winter, 2007). Post-secularism recognizes that "religion maintains a public influence and relevance, while the secularistic certainty that religion will disappear worldwide in the course of modernization is losing ground" (Habermas, 2008). In 2008, Jürgen Habermas argued that modernity no longer implies an alignment with secularism, observing that Western societies have drawn on Judeo-Christian values to shape their own morality and ethics. This has significant implications for the framing of heritage praxis, as it forces an acknowledgement of the need for political and social engagement with religious voices that have been shaping landscapes and practices all along.

The ways in which religious traditions have been engaged in the preservation and collecting practices of museums, archaeological sites, architectural, historical, and contemporary places and traditions aligns with Zeruvabel's (2018) framing of dichotomies. A concern with religion and secularism in heritage studies brings to focus the elusiveness of heritage value in general, not just in relation to the intimacy of faith-based forms of knowledge that a heritage of religion may contain. Spearheading this epistemic transformation, Denis Byrne has convincingly argued that heritage is, in fact, encrypted terrain, and "no amount of archaeological skill or 'sensibility' will be enough to decode it" (2007: xii). His work across various Southeast Asian contexts disrupts the idea that heritage value exists on the surface as an observable and measurable quality, putting to test our ability to "read" cultural landscapes, objects, and practices that are largely constructed on traces of meaning often suppressed and buried underground. This redirection gives way to a study of heritage value that is contained in material and immaterial *traces* (cf. Morgan, 2010). This is a redirection from a methodological emphasis on measurable authenticity and integrity that is reflected in the privileging of visual, aesthetic, and architectural properties, languages, and archives. Yet, rather than simply de-privileging visuality, it is important to recognize that approaching the study of heritage and religion from the perspective of religious traditions themselves is to recognize that "the gaze" is transformative to believers in ways that are not easily transferable to nonbelievers, as is true for other operations of the sensorium. David Morgan describes this gaze as "the manner in which a way of seeing invests an image, a viewer, or an act of viewing with spiritual significance" (2005: 3–4). From the perspective of believers, then, visuality is essential. For example, Hillary Kaell's (2017) ethnographic fieldwork on the preservation of wayside crosses of Quebec captures a familiar tension. While caretakers' sentiments may be articulated in historical terms in order to ascribe the crosses to a Catholic *patrimoine* (heritage), it is in the act of *seeing* that caretaking begins. The recognition of "ambient faith," that is, religiosity that filters in and out of sensory and conscious space (Kaell, 2017; cf. Engelke, 2012), helps describe the caretakers' perspective in her work: people do not translate every sensation into discourse, "nor do they want to" (Kaell, 2017: 132; see also Morgan, 2010: 135).

Recognizing the invisible universe surrounding religious objects that is energized and animated by various forms of divine and supernatural powers offers productive ontological detachment from dominant heritage views and practices (Byrne, 2004, 2014). The fact that the landscapes, practices, and voices of the divine have been present all along confirms that modern heritage preservation approaches are ill-equipped to embark on the study of discursive invisibility of this magnitude. Increasing calls for the establishment of ethnographic heritage approaches in the lifetime of a heritage preservation discipline are plenty (Low 2002; Lafrenz-Samuels, 2018). These not only seek to diversify forms of engagement with heritage stakeholders through collaboration, but they also call for diversifying the types of data that are used to constitute practices and traditions of heritage preservation. The goal remains to recognize the less privileged dimensions in the construction of heritage and the dynamic and heterogeneous characteristics of contemporary heritage archives as demonstrated through methodological contributions from anthropology, folklore, and history, among others. For some time now, a concern with cosmopolitan heritage ethics has argued in support of multi-scalar engagements that recognize the obligations that heritage experts have toward broader human realities and experiences, which are not always preservationist in ethos (Meskell, 2009: 4). A "collaborative turn" (Colwell-Chanthaphonh and Ferguson, 2008: 3) in archaeological and museum practice saw a marked increase in community-oriented approaches and collaborative practices through the 1990s. This collaborative turn was not simply discursive but also reflected in the drafting of new legal instruments and a measurable increase in public and participatory work. For example, in the United States, the Native American Graves Protection and Repatriation Act (NAGPRA) affords tribes the right to repatriate Native American cultural items that meet certain criteria, including human remains, associated and unassociated funerary objects, cultural patrimony, and sacred items (NPS, 2020).

However, legal recognition and disciplinary attitudes to forms of authority are not always the same. In April of 2021, controversy erupted across the Society for American Archaeology (SAA) over a featured presentation at their virtual annual meeting. The paper, "Has Creationism Crept Back in Archaeology?" coauthored by anthropologist Elizabeth Weiss and former attorney James Springer, argued against NAGPRA's legal protections for Native American remains and cultural artifacts. Echoing the arguments articulated in their coauthored book (Weiss and Springer, 2020), they claim that such protection gives "control of research over to contemporary American Indian communities" (Wade, 2021), depriving the scientific community of certain types of research on account of religious beliefs. A significant portion of the archaeological community attached to the SAA called out these statements as an attack on indigenous rights through racist and anti-religious claims surrounding repatriation. Weiss and Springer's (2021) work is founded on the overarching claim that the practices and approaches that support repatriation are informed by an anti-science stance. The authors themselves responded to what they defined as "hysteria" over their SAA presentation, claiming that they "were making a case for science and objective knowledge over the religious literalism of creationism" (Springer and Weiss, 2021). In their view, the observance of religious traditions by the archaeological community denigrates scientific knowledge. In critiquing the validity of religious traditions that can inform the construction of archaeological data, Weiss and Springer (2021) also undermine the epistemological journey that has taken the fields of archaeology and heritage away from monolithic interpretations of the complexity of human experiences in the landscape and material culture and toward operationalizing multivocality in heritage preservation discourse and practice. The embrace of a "fundamentalism of the Enlightenment" (Habermas, 2008: 24) that permeates Weiss and Springer's position is what social archaeologists, from Ian Hodder ("whose rationality?" 1998) to Denis Byrne ("fortress of rationality," 2009), forewarned. Challenging the distinction between fact (an external reality) and fetish (a foolish belief), Bruno Latour proposes that "it must be possible to make a place for the divinities again, provided that we modify the space in which they might be deployed" (2010: 39). The recent SAA showdown reveals precisely why religious practice needs to be normalized in the space of affective experiences of heritage value and the associated construction of heritage ethics.

The centrality of affectivity in heritage value has, surprisingly, skirted around the subject of religious experience effectively. A concern with affect recognizes that heritage value resides in and is constituted by diverse fabrics and spaces and can be understood as a multi-sensorial experience (cf. Coelho, 2019). While affectivity has been invested in the theoretical potentialities of distinguishing between "ways of seeing" and "ways of being" (Tolia-Kelly, Waterton, and Watson, 2016: 4), a further epistemic exploration needs to be addressed in methodological approaches for the study and management of heritage preservation. A rare example of a practical recognition of affectivity in relation to religious traditions is documented by Simon Warrack, a conservator working on the restoration of the statue of Ta Reach in Angkor Wat as part of the German Apsara Conservation Project. Recognizing the voice of the spirit as a key stakeholder in the spiritual integrity of a religious monument is rare in a discipline that has grown out of scientific concerns. Warrack (2011) demonstrates how the spirit itself is involved in the consultation process that dictates conservation decisions and how the wishes of the spirit and its community can be taken into consideration. Such an example marks a shift in approaches to preservation that recognize a belief in the numinous, that is, the inner divinity or supernatural force, a belief that exists not merely alongside modernity but in concert with it and may involve practices and practitioners that run contrary to and compete with a conservation ethic over physical fabric (Byrne, 2019: 3–4). The scarcity of this type of case study is evidence that secularist instruments in heritage discourse have given shape to methodological trajectories that exclude the spirits in seemingly irreversible ways that do not coincidentally mirror imperial processes. Established approaches for the study and preservation of heritage are not easily retrofitted with religious practice. The task, therefore, is to think beyond the confines of existing approaches in heritage and preservation. This reflection is evident at two familiar epistemic points that have manifested in the field and extend beyond the context of a heritage of religion: the construction of heritage voices and the curation of heritage data.

Calls for coparticipatory heritage preservation that aim to expand the diversity and influence of stakeholders in heritage preservation are not new but continue to gain sophistication and provide a foundation for a better engagement with religious communities and leaders. Contemporary appeals for collaboration make a distinction between working *with* and working *for* a particular stakeholder group, recognizing and planning for shared as well as non-shared interests, such as research and repatriation claims (Meloche, Spake, and Nichols, 2020). This shift in attitudes also takes seriously the different roles that populate the heritage economy. For example, archaeologist Mudit Trivedi confronts a public archaeology in India that has remained insensitive to a counter-public, that is, public excluded from the work of public engagement through incarceration and punishment in the name of the greater archaeological common good (Trivedi, 2019: 22). Echoing a rapprochement with unofficial and illegal archaeological extractions across the UK (Lewis, 2016), these calls for a reconciliation of diametrically opposed stakeholder agendas are also championed by museum specialists, leaders, and legal scholars. Similarly, they argue in favor of collaborating with collectors of illicit antiquities for the greater good (Pearlstein, 2014; Marlowe, 2017; Vikan, 2017). A reexamination of the grounds for exclusion in shifting legal and moral landscapes of care for heritage resources gives way to radical possibilities for a public engagement (González-Ruibal, González, and Criado-Boado, 2018), and a redefinition of what constitutes the fabric of heritage value itself. On this topic, Denis Byrne emphasizes that "devotees are not distant or passive observers of the miraculous performativity of things" (Byrne, 2019: 6). The implications for methodological approaches in critical heritage studies are ample. Specifically, this epistemological vantage point authorizes stakeholders and scholars themselves to be part of an intimate and experiential construction of knowledge. The specter of empiricism that is so strongly attached to the study of heritage preservation has resulted in an interesting contrast in any encounter with indigeneity that contains religious traditions: whereby non-disciplinary local stakeholders are expected and sometimes allowed to possess knowledge that transcends the limits of empiricism, researchers themselves are expected to capture and assess this knowledge from a scientific point of view. In other words, researchers, regardless of their own beliefs and experiences, are expected to brandish the flag of empiricism.

This is an argument in support of studying counter-archives through counter-methodologies. For example, working at the intersection of anthropology and contemporary art, George Tebogo Mahashe (2019) argues that the study of "alternative" archives requires a different methodological sensitivity. His work encourages scholars who are marginalized from dominant forms of knowledge production by the forces of colonialism to engage with the archive from their own point of view. His study of rumor and dreaming, topics that are often dismissed or stigmatized, advocates for methodological approaches that redraw the limits of cultural studies. These include the practice of walkabout (2020) and dreaming (2019), among other creative processes that also allow the researcher to understand and confront the opacity of their subjectivity and subjects of study – what Latour (2010) refers to as "factish" knowledge, neither fact nor fetish. In doing so, Mahashe also calls attention to the literacies that alternative modes of capture require. These literacies are not fostered by the dominant forms of training in the study and management of heritage. Instead, a significant part of building this literacy involves recognizing the validity of religious beliefs, or lack thereof, within the epistemological frameworks of research, researched, and researcher.

The fostering of alternative literacies to support the post-secular study and management of heritage should be done in a transformative rather than merely additive way and through intentional disciplinary reconfigurations. If the critical heritage turn is committed to revolting against the secularist undertones that persist in the field, both discursively and practically, it must go beyond a blanket call for more anthropological engagements. Just as the field has increasingly recognized new and diverse dimensions of heritage value over the decades, the goal should be *to discipline* "religion" into the center, and not the precarious margins, of heritage and preservation studies. As I discuss throughout this Element, expanding into new dimensions means embracing two interrelated interventions. First, it is necessary to underscore the distinction between *different ways of seeing a heritage* and *seeing different heritages*. Second, it is important to recognize that *collecting new voices* and *letting them operate within their own ontologies* are different enterprises. In this way, experts in the field may capture different encounters between a heritage object and its heritage subjects in more sophisticated detail. Going beyond the dichotomizing discourses of iconoclasm, destruction, and neglect, a study of heritage that is attentive to the realms of religious tradition and belief can transform the discipline into one concerned with safeguarding agency, ingenuity, and hybridity.

References

Abraham, J. (2005). Archaeology and Politics: A Case Study of the Ayodhya Issue. *Material Religion*, **1**(2), 253–260.

Abu-Lughod, L. (1991). Writing against Culture. In R. G. Fox, ed., *Recapturing Anthropology: Working in the Present*. Santa Fe: School of American Research Press, pp. 137–162.

Adams, C. (1998). Japan's Ise Shrine and Its Thirteen-Hundred-Year-Old Reconstruction Tradition. *Journal of Architectural Education*, **52**(1), 49–60.

Akagawa, N. (2015). Rethinking the Global Heritage Discourse – Overcoming "East" and "West"? *International Journal of Heritage Studies*, **22**(1), 14–25.

Alrawaibah, A. (2014). Archaeological Site Management in the Kingdom of Saudi Arabia: Protection or Isolation? In K. Exell and T. Rico, eds., *Cultural Heritage in the Arabian Peninsula: Debates, Discourses and Practices*. Farnham: Taylor and Francis, pp. 143–156.

Anderson, B. (1983). *Imagined Communities: Reflections on the Origin and Spread of Nationalism*. London: Verso.

Antohin, A. S. (2019). Preserving the Intangible: Orthodox Christian Approaches to Spiritual Heritage. *Religions*, **10**(36), 1–12.

Arthur, C. (2000). Exhibiting the Sacred. In C. Paine, ed., *Godly Things: Museums, Objects and Religion*. New York: Leicester University Press, pp. 1–27.

Asad, T. (1993). *Genealogies of Religion: Disciplines and Reasons of Power in Christianity and Islam*. Baltimore: The John Hopkins University Press, pp. 27–54.

Aston, M. (1973). English Ruins and English History: The Dissolution and the Sense of the Past. *Journal of the Warburg and Courtauld Institutes*, **36**(1973), 231–255.

Atkin, N. (1991). The Politics of Legality: The Religious Orders in France, 1901–45. In F. Tallett and N. Atkin, eds., *Religion, Society and Politics in France since 1789*. London and Rio Grande: The Hambledon Press, pp. 149–165.

Australia ICOMOS (1988). *Code on the Ethics of Co-existence in Conserving Significant Places*. https://australia.icomos.org/wp-content/uploads/Code-on-the-Ethics-of-Co-existence.pdf.

Australia ICOMOS (1999). *The Burra Charter*. https://australia.icomos.org/wp-content/uploads/BURRA_CHARTER.pdf.

Baillie, B. and Chippindale, C. (2007). Tangible-Intangible Cultural Heritage: A Sustainable Dichotomy? The 7th Annual Cambridge Heritage Seminar, 13 May 2006. McDonald Institute for Archaeological Research, University of Cambridge, UK. *Conservation and Management of Archaeological Sites*, **8**, 174–176.

Barkan, E. and Barkey, K. (2015). *Choreographies of Shared Sacred Sites: Religion, Politics, and Conflict Resolution*. New York: Columbia University Press.

Benjamin, W. (1992). *Illuminations*. London: Fontana.

Berliner, D. (2013). Editorial Statement: Heritage and the Sacred: Introduction. *Material Religion: The Journal of Objects, Art and Belief*, **9**, 274–280.

Bhambra, G. K. (2014). Postcolonial and Decolonial Dialogues. *Postcolonial Studies*, **17**(2), 115–121.

Bigelow, A. (2010). *Sharing the Sacred: Practising Pluralism in Muslim North India*. Oxford: Oxford University Press.

Bowler, P. J. (2014). From Agnosticism to Rationalism: Evolutionary Biologists, the Rationalist Press Association, and Early Twentieth-Century Scientific Naturalism. In G. Dawson and B. Lightman, eds., *Victorian Scientific Naturalism: Community, Identity, Continuity*. Chicago and London: University of Chicago Press, pp. 309–326.

Bowman, G. (2012). Introduction: Sharing the Sacra. In G. Bowman, ed., *Sharing the Sacra: The Politics and Pragmatics of Inter-communal Relations around Holy Places*. New York and Oxford: Berghahn Books, pp. 1–9.

Brandi, C. (2005). *Theory of Restoration*. Firenze and Rome: Istituto Centrale per il Restauro.

Britton, K. C. (2010). The Case for Sacred Architecture. In K. C. Britton, ed., *Constructing the Ineffable: Contemporary Sacred Architecture*. New Haven: Yale University Press, pp. 12–23.

Brumann, C. and Berliner, D. (2016). Introduction: UNESCO World Heritage – Grounded? In C. Brumann and D. Berliner, eds., *World Heritage on the Ground: Ethnographic Perspectives*. New York: Berghahn Books, pp. 1–34.

Brusius, M. and Dukelgrün, T. (2016). Photography, Antiquity, Scholarship. *History of Photography*, **40**(3), 139.

Buchli, V. (2002). *The Material Culture Reader*. Oxford: Berg.

Buggeln, G. T. (2012). Museum Space and the Experience of the Sacred. *Material Religion: The Journal of Objects, Art and Belief*, **8**(1), 30–50.

Bumbaru, D. (2008). Religious Heritage and Sacred Places. *ICOMOS News*, **17**, 6–7.

Burris, J. P. (2001). *Exhibiting Religion: Colonialism and Spectacle at International Expositions 1851–1893*. Charlottesville and London: University Press of Virginia.

Byrne, D. (1991). Western Hegemony in Archaeological Heritage Management. *History and Anthropology*, **5**, 269–276.

Byrne, D. (1995). Buddhist Stupa and Thai Social Practice. *World Archaeology*, **27**(2), 266–281.

Byrne, D. (2004). Chartering Heritage in Asia's Post-modern World Conservation. *The Getty Conservation Institute Newsletter*, **19**(2), 16–19.

Byrne, D. (2006). Archaeology and the Fortress of Rationality. In L. Meskell, ed., *Cosmopolitan Archaeologies*. Raleigh: Duke University Press, pp. 68–88.

Byrne, D. (2007). *Surface Collection: Archaeological Travels in Southeast Asia*. Lanham: Altamira Press.

Byrne, D. 2009. Archaeology and the Fortress of Rationality. In Cosmopolitan Archaeologies. Edited by Lynn Meskell. Durham: Duke University Press, pp. 68-88

Byrne, D. (2014). *Counterheritage: Critical Perspectives on Heritage Conservation in Asia*. London and New York: Routledge.

Byrne, D. (2019). Prospects for a Postsecular Heritage Practice: Convergences between Posthumanism and Popular Religious Practice in Asia. *Religions*, **10**(7), 436.

Byrne, D. and Nugent, M. (2004). *Mapping Attachment: A Spatial Approach to Aboriginal Post-contact Heritage*. Hurtsville: Department of Environment and Conservation.

Cantor, G. (2011). *Religion and the Great Exhibition of 1851*. Oxford: Oxford University Press.

Caple, C. (2000). *Conservation Skills: Judgement, Method, and Decision Making*. Abingdon: Routledge.

Casanova, J. (2009). The Secular and Secularisms. *Social Research*, **76**(4), 1049–1066.

Chidester, D. (2018). *Religion: Material Dynamics*. Berkeley: University of California Press.

Clavir, M. (1996). Reflections on Changes in Museums and the Conservation of Collections from Indigenous Peoples. *Journal of the American Institute of Conservation*, **35**(2), 43–46.

Clavir, M. (2002). *Preserving What Is Valued: Museums, Conservation and First Nations*. Vancouver and Toronto: UBC Press.

Cleere, H. (2001). The Uneasy Bedfellows: Universality and Cultural Heritage. In R. Layton, J. Thomas, and P. G. Stone, eds., *Destruction and Conservation of Cultural Property*. London and New York: Routledge, pp. 22–29.

Coelho, R. G. (2019). An Archaeology of Decolonization: Imperial Intimacies in Contemporary Lisbon. *Journal of Social Archaeology*, **19**(2), 181–205.

Colwell-Chanthaphonh, C. and Ferguson, T. J. (2008). Introduction: The Collaborative Continuum. In Colwell-Chanthaphonh, C. and Ferguson, T. J., eds., *Collaboration in Archaeological Practice: Engaging Descendant Communities*. Walnut Creek: Altamira Press, pp. 1–32.

Council of Europe (2000). Recommendation 1484: Management of Cathedrals and Other Major Religious Buildings in Use. In *European Cultural Heritage – Volume I, Intergovernmental Co-operation: Collected Texts*. Strasbourg: Council of Europe, pp. 347–350.

de Vries, H. (2001). In Media Res: Global Religion, Public Sphere, and the Task of Contemporary Comparative Religious Studies. In H. De Vries and S. Weber, eds., *Religion and Media*. Stanford: Stanford University Press, pp. 3–42.

de Vries, H., ed. (2008). *Religion: Beyond a Concept*. New York: Fordham University Press.

Di Giovine, M. A. and Choe, J. (2019). Geographies of Religion and Spirituality: Pilgrimage beyond the "Officially" Sacred. *Tourism Geographie*, **21**(3), 361–383.

Di Giovine, M. A. and Garcia-Fuentes, J. M. (2016). Sites of Pilgrimage, Sites of Heritage: An Exploratory Introduction. *International Journal of Tourism Anthropology*, **5**(1/2), 1–23.

Duncan, C. (1995). *Civilizing Rituals: Inside Public Art Museums*. London: Routledge.

Eade, J. (2009). Power and Sacred Art. In M. Snodin and N. Llewellyn, eds., *Baroque 1620–1800: Style in the Age of Magnificence*. London: V&A, pp. 241–256.

Elias, J. (2007). (Un)making Idolatry: From Mecca to Bamiyan, Future Anterior. *Journal of Historic Preservation, History, Theory and Criticism*, **4**(2), 13–29.

Engelke, M. (2012). Angels in Swindon: Public Religion and Ambient Faith in England. *American Ethnologist*, **39**(1), 155–170.

Flood, F. B. (2002). Between Cult and Culture: Bamiyan, Islamic Iconoclasm, and the Museum. *The Art Bulletin*, **84**(4), 641–659.

Foxlee, J. (2009). Meaningful Rocks: The Sorry Rock Phenomenon at Uluru-Kata Tjuta National Park. *Material Religion: The Journal of Objects, Art and Belief*, **5**(1), 123–124.

Fricker, M. (2007). *Epistemic Injustice: Power and the Ethics of Knowing.* Oxford: Oxford University Press.

Geertz, C. (1966). Religion as a Cultural System. In B. Michael, ed., *Anthropological Approaches to the Study of Religion.* London: Tavistock, pp. 1–46.

Goldberger, P. (2010). Epilogue: On the Relevance of Sacred Architecture Today. In K. C. Britton, ed., *Constructing the Ineffable: Contemporary Sacred Architecture.* New Haven: Yale University Press, pp. 222–31.

Goldstein, E. (2011). Redeeming Holy Wisdom: Britain and St. Sophia. In M. Hall, ed., *Towards World Heritage: International Origins of the Preservation Movement 1870–1930.* Farnham: Routledge, pp. 45–62.

González-Ruibal, A., González, P., and Criado-Boado, F. (2018). Against Reactionary Populism: Towards a New Public Archaeology. *Antiquity,* **92** (362), 507–515.

Goodale, M. (2018). *Letters to the Contrary: A Curated History of the UNESCO Human Rights Survey.* Stanford: Stanford University Press.

Habermas, Jürgen. "Notes on Post-Secular Society." *New Perspectives Quarterly* 25, no. 4 (2008): 17–29.

Hafstein, V. T. (2018). *Making Intangible Heritage: El Condor Pasa and Other Stories from UNESCO.* Bloomington: Indiana University Press.

Hafstein, V. T. and Skrydstrup, M. (2020). *Patrimonialities: Heritage vs. Property.* Cambridge: Cambridge University Press.

Hall, M. (2011). Introduction: Towards World Heritage. In Hall, M., ed., *Towards World Heritage: International Origins of the Preservation Movement 1870–1930.* London: Routledge, pp. 1–19.

Hamilakis, Y. and Infantidis, F. (2015). The Photographic and the Archaeological: The "Other Acropolis." In P. Carabott, Y. Hamilakis, and E. Papargyriou, eds., *Camera Graeca: Photographs, Narratives, Materialities.* Farnham: Ashgate, pp. 133–157.

Harrison, R. (2013). *Heritage: Critical Approaches.* London: Routledge.

Harrison, R. (2016). World Heritage Listing and the Globalization of the Endangerment Sensibility. In F. Vidal and N. Dias, eds., *Endangerment, Biodiversity and Culture.* Abingdon and New York: Routledge, pp. 195–217.

Hassner, R. E. (2009). *War on Sacred Grounds.* Ithaca: Cornell University Press.

Hayes, M. (2019). On the Origins of Alois Riegl's Conservation Theory. *Journal of the American Institute for Conservation,* **58**(3), 132–143.

Hertzfeld, M. (2006). Spatial Cleansing: Monumental Vacuity and the Idea of the West. *Journal of Material Culture,* **11**(1/2), 127–149.

Hodder, I. (1998). Whose Rationality? A Response to Fekri Hassan. *Antiquity*, **72**(275), 213–217.

Hoggart, R. (1978). *An Idea and Its Servants: UNESCO from within*. New York: Oxford University Press.

Holtorf, C. and Schadla-Hall, T. (1999). Age as Artefact: On Archaeological Authenticity. *European Journal of Archaeology*, **2**(2), 229–247.

Hubert, J. (1994). Sacred Beliefs and Beliefs of Sacredness. In D. Carmichael, J. Hubert, B. Reeves, and A. Schance, eds., *Sacred Sites, Sacred Places*. Abingdon: Routledge, pp. 9–19.

Huxley, J. (2010). *UNESCO: Its Purpose and Philosophy. Facsimiles of English and French Editions of this Visionary Policy Document*. London: Euston Grove Press.

ICOMOS (1965). International Charter for the Conservation and Restoration of Monuments and Sites (The Venice Charter 1964). *IInd International Congress of Architects and Technicians of Historic Monuments, Venice, 1964*. www.icomos.org/charters/venice_e.pdf.

ICOMOS (1994). *The Nara Document on Authenticity*. www.icomos.org/charters/nara-e.pdf.

ICOMOS (1996). *Advisory Body Evaluation: World Heritage List – Hiroshima – No 775*. http://whc.unesco.org/archive/advisory_body_evaluation/775.pdf.

ICOMOS (2004). The World Heritage List: Filling the Gaps – An action Plan for the Future. *An Analysis by ICOMOS*. Paris.

ICOMOS (2008a). *Québec Declaration on the Preservation of the Spirit of a Place*. https://whc.unesco.org/uploads/activities/documents/activity-646-2.pdf.

ICOMOS (2008b). The International Day for Monuments and Sites: Religious heritage and Sacred Places. *ICOMOS Secretariat Memo*. www.icomos.org/18thapril/2008/18042008-e.pdf.

ICOMOS. 2011. 17th General Assembly of ICOMOS. Paris, France 27 November to 2 December 2011. https://whc.unesco.org/uploads/activities/documents/activity-646-1.pdf

Isnart, C. and Cerezales, N. (2020). Introduction. In Isnart, C. and Cerezales, N., eds., *The Religious Heritage Complex: Legacy, Conservation, and Christianity*. London: Bloomsbury, pp. 1–13.

Jager, C. (2015). *Unquiet Things: Secularism in the Romantic Age*. Philadelphia: University of Pennsylvania Press.

Jensen, U. J. (2000). Cultural Heritage, Liberal Education, and Human Flourishing. In E. Avrami, R. Mason, and M. de la Torre, eds., *Values and*

Heritage Conservation. Los Angeles: Getty Conservation Institute, pp. 38–43.

Jokilehto, J. (2012). *A History of Architectural Conservation*. London and New York: Routledge.

Joy, C. (2012). *The Politics of Heritage Management in Mali: From UNESCO to Djenné*. London: Routledge.

Kaell, H. (2017). Seeing the Invisible: Ambient Catholicism on the Side of the Road. *Journal of the American Academy of Religion*, **85**(1), 136–167.

Kaell, H. (2019). Marking Memory: Heritage Work and Devotional Labor at Quebec's Croix de Chemin. In K. Norget, ed., *The Anthropology of Catholicism: A Reader*. Berkeley: University Press of California, pp. 122–138.

Karlström, A. (2005). Spiritual Materiality: Heritage Preservation in a Buddhist World? *Journal of Social Archaeology*, **5**(3), 338–355.

Karlström, A. (2013). Spirits and the Ever-Changing Heritage. *Material Religion*, **9**(3), 395–399.

Keane, W. (2006). Anxious Trascendence. In F. Cannell, ed., *The Anthropology of Christianity*. Durham: Duke University Press, pp. 308–324.

Keane, W. (2018). On Semiotic Ideology. *Signs and Society*, **6**(1), 64–87.

Kitagawa, J. M. (1993). The 1893 World's Parliament of Religions and Its Legacy. In E. J. Ziolkowski, ed., *A Museum of Faiths: Histories and Legacies of the 1893 World's Parliament of Religions*. Atlanta: Scholars Press, pp. 185–187.

Kreps, C. F. (2003). *Liberating Culture: Cross-Cultural Perspectives on Museums, Curation, and Heritage Preservation*. London: Routledge.

Kreps, C. F. (2005). Indigenous Curation as Intangible Cultural Heritage: Thoughts on the Relevance of the 2003 UNESCO Convention. *Theorizing Cultural Heritage*, **1**(2), 3–8.

Kreps, C. F. and MacDonald, S. (2006). Non-Western Models of Museums and Curation in Cross-Cultural Perspective. In Sharon Macdonald, ed., *A Companion to Museum Studies*. Oxford: Blackwell, pp. 457–472.

Labadi, S. (2005). A Review of the Global Strategy for a Balanced Representative and Credible World Heritage List 1994–2004. *Conservation and Management of Archaeological Sites*, **7**, 89–102.

Labadi, S. "Representations of the Nation and Cultural Diversity in Discourses on World Heritage." *Journal of Social Archaeology* 7, no. 2 (2007): 147–70.

Lachman, C. (2014). Buddhism: Image as Icon, Image as Art. In F. Burch Brown, ed., *The Oxford Handbook of Religion and the Arts*. Oxford: Oxford University Press, pp. 367–378.

Lafrenz Samuels, K. (2018). *Mobilizing Heritage: Anthropological Practice and Transnational Prospects*. Gainesville: University Press of Florida.

Lafrenz-Samuels, K. and Rico, T. (2015). *Heritage Keywords: Rhetoric and Redescription in Cultural Heritage*. Boulder: University Press of Colorado.

Lamprakos, M. (2014). Riegl's "Modern Cult of Monuments" and the Problem of Value. *Change Over Time*, **4**(2), 418–435.

Latour, B. (2010). *On the Modern Cult of the Factish Gods*. Durham: Duke University Press.

Lecourt, S. (2018). *Cultivating Belief: Victorian Anthropology, Liberal Aesthetics, and the Secular Imagination*. Oxford: Oxford University Press.

Lewis, B. (1990). The Roots of Muslim Rage. *The Atlantic*, **266**(3), 47–60.

Lewis, M. (2016). A Detectorist's Utopia? Archaeology and Metal-Detecting in England and Wales. *Open Archaeology*, **2**, 127–139.

Lincoln, B. (1996). Theses on Method. *Method & Theory in the Study of Religion*, **8**(3), 225–227.

Low, S. (2002). Anthropological-Ethnographic Methods for the Assessment of Cultural Values in Heritage Conservation. In M. de la Torre, ed., *Assessing the Values of Cultural Heritage*. Los Angeles: Getty Conservation Institute, pp. 31–50.

Lowenthal, D. (1998). *The Heritage Crusade and the Spoils of History*. Cambridge: Cambridge University Press.

Mahashe, G. T. (2019). *MaBareBare: A Rumour of a Dream*. PhD Thesis. Michaelis School of Art University of Cape Town, South Africa.

Mahashe, G. T. (2020). Walking Towards a Camera Obscura/Marcher vers une Chambre Obscure. *Critical African Studies*, **12**(2), 218–236.

Marijnissen, R. H. (2015). Degradation, Conservation, and Restoration of Works of Art: Historical Overview. In N. Stanley Prince, M. Kirby Talley Jr., and A. Melucco Vaccarro, eds., *Historical and Philosophical Issues in the Conservation of Cultural Heritage*. Los Angeles: Getty Conservation Institute, pp. 275–280.

Marlowe, E. (2017). American Museums First? A Response to Gary Vikan. *W86th Notes from the Field*. www.west86th.bgc.bard.edu/responses/american-museums-first-a-response-to-gary-vikan/.

Meloche, C. H., Spake, L., and Nichols, K. L. (2020). Introduction: Working Together to Do Better. In *Working with and for Ancestors: Collaboration in the Care and Study of Ancestral Remains*. New York: Routledge, pp. 1–19.

Meskell, L. (2002). Negative Heritage and Past Mastering in Archaeology. *Anthropological Quarterly*, **75**(3), 557–574.

Meskell, L. (2009). Introduction: Cosmopolitan Heritage Ethics. In L. Meskell, ed., *Cosmopolitan Archaeologies*. Durham: Duke University Press, pp. 1–27.

Meskell, L. (2018). *A Future in Ruins: UNESCO, World Heritage, and the Dream of Peace*. Oxford: Oxford University Press.

Meyer, B. (2008). Materializing Religion: Material Religion. *The Journal of Objects, Art and Belief*, **4**(2), 226–227.

Meyer, B. and de Witte, M. (2013). Heritage and the Sacred: Introduction, Material Religion. *The Journal of Objects, Art and Belief*, **9**(3), 274–281.

Meyer, B. and Houtman, D. (2012). Introduction: Material Religion- How Things Matter. In *Things: Religion and the Question of Materiality*. New York: Fordham University Press, pp. 1–23.

Meyer, B., Morgan, D., Paine, C., and Plate, S. B. (2010). The Origins and Mission of Material Religion. *Religion*, **40**(3), 209.

Miura, K. (2005). Conservation of a "Living Heritage Site": A Contradiction in Terms? A Case Study of Angkor World Heritage Site. *Conservation and Management of Archaeological Sites*, **7**(1), 3–18.

Miura, K. (2007). A Note on the Current Impact of Tourism on Angkor and Its Environs. *Conservation and Management of Archaeological Sites*, **8**(1), 132–135.

Morgan, D. (2005). *The Sacred Gaze: Religious Visual Culture in Theory and in Practice*. Berkeley: University of California Press.

Morgan, D. (2010). Materiality, Social Analysis, and the study of Religion. In D. Morgan, ed., *Religion and Material Culture: The Matter of Belief*. New York: Routledge, pp. 55–74.

Mossallam, A. (2012). *Hikāyāt Sha'b: Stories of Peoplehood, Nasserism, Popular Politics and Songs in Egypt 1956–1973*. PhD Thesis. Department of Government, London School of Economics and Political Science.

NPS (2020). *Native American Graves Protection and Repatriation Act. Glossary*. www.nps.gov/subjects/nagpra/glossary.htm.

Olsen, B. (2010). *In Defense of Things: Archaeology and the Ontology of Objects*. Lanham: Altamira Press.

Paine, C. (2013). *Religious Objects in Museums: Private Lives and Public Duties*. London: Bloomsbury Academic.

Pearlstein, W. J. (2014). White Paper: A Proposal to Reform US Law and Policy Relating to the International Exchange of Cultural Property. *Cardozo Arts & Entertainment Law Journal*, **32**(3), 561–650.

Pels, P. (2008). The Modern Fear of Matter: Reflections on the Protestantism of Victorian Science. *Material Religion: The Journal of Objects, Art and Belief*, **4**(3), 264–283.

Pels, P. (2012). The Modern Fear of Matter: Reflections on the Protestantism of Victorian Science. In B. Meyer and D. Houtman, eds., *Things: Religion and the Question of Materiality*. New York: Fordham University Press, pp. 27–39.

Pomian, K. (1990). *Collectors and Curiosities: Paris and Venice, 1500–1800.* Cambridge: Polity Press.

Rausch, C. (2017). *Global Heritage Assemblages: Development and Modern Architecture in Africa.* New York and London: Routledge.

Rico, T. 2008. "'Negative Heritage': The Place of Conflict in World Heritage," *Conservation and Management of Archaeological Sites* 10(4): 344–352.

Rico, T. (2015). Heritage at Risk: The Authority and Autonomy of a Dominant Framework. In K. Lafrenz-Samuels and T. Rico, eds., *Heritage Keywords: Rhetoric and Redescription in Cultural Heritage.* Boulder: University Press of Colorado, pp. 147–162.

Rico, T. (2016). *Constructing Destruction: Heritage Narratives in the Tsunami City.* London and New York: Routledge.

Rico, T. (2017). Stakeholder in Practice: "Us," "Them," and the Problem of Expertise. In C. Hillerdal, A. Karlström, and C. Ojala, eds., *Archaeologies of "Us" and "Them": Debating the Politics of Ethnicity and Indigeneity in Archaeology and Heritage Discourse.* Abingdon and New York: Routledge, pp. 38–52.

Rico. T. (2019). Islam, Heritage, and Preservation: An Untidy Tradition, Material Religion. *The Journal of Objects, Art and Belief: Heritage, Islam and the Vernacular,* **15**(2), 148–163.

Rico, T. (2020). Is There an "Islamic" Practice for the Preservation of Cultural Heritage? In B. Walker, T. Insoll, and C. Fenwick, eds., *The Oxford Handbook of Islamic Archaeology.* Oxford: Oxford University Press.

Rico, T. and Lababidi, R. (2017). Extremism in Contemporary Heritage Debates about Islam: Future Anterior. *Journal of Historic Preservation, History, Theory and Criticism. Preservation and War,* **14**(1), 94–105.

Riegl, A. (1982). The Modern Cult of Monuments: Its Character and Its Origin. *Oppositions,* **25**, 21–51.

Rots, A. P. (2019). World Heritage, Secularisation, and the New "Public Sacred" in East Asia. *Journal of Religion in Japan,* **8**(1/3), 151–178.

Rudolff, B. 2006. *'Intangible' and 'tangible' heritage: A Topology of Culture in Contexts of Faith.* PhD thesis, Institute of Geography, Faculty for Chemistry, Pharmacy and Geo-sciences, Johannes Gutenberg-University of Mainz, Germany.

Rudolff, B. (2010). *"Intangible" and "Tangible" Heritage: A Topology of Culture in Contexts of Faith.* Bonn: Scientia Bonnensis.

Ruskin, J. (1890). *The Seven Lamps of Architecture.* New York: John Wiley.

Saifi, Y. and Yüceer, H. (2013). Maintaining the Absent Other: The Re-use of Religious Heritage Sites in Conflicts. *International Journal of Heritage Studies,* **19**(7), 749–763.

Schildgen, B. D. (2008). *Heritage or Heresy: Preservation and Destruction of Religious Art and Architecture in Europe*. New York: Palgrave.

Schnapp, A. (1996). *The Discovery of the Past: The Origins of Archaeology*. London: British Museum Press.

Shanks, M. and Svabo, C. (2013). Archeology and Photography: A Pragmatology. In A. Gonzáles-Ruibal, ed., *Reclaiming Archaeology: Beyond the Tropes of Modernity*. New York: Routledge, pp. 89–102.

Shaw, J. (2002). Ayohdya's Sacred Landscape: Ritual Memory, Politics and Archaeological "Fact." *Antiquity*, **74**(285), 673–700.

Sherman, D. J. (1989). *Worthy Monuments: Art Museums and the Politics of Culture in Nineteenth-Century France*. Cambridge, MA: Harvard University Press.

Sherman, D. J. (1999). *The Construction of Memory in Interwar France*. Chicago and London: University of Chicago Press.

Silverman, H. and Ruggles, D. F. (2007). Cultural Heritage and Human Rights. In H. Silverman and D. F. Ruggles, eds., *Cultural Heritage and Human Rights*. New York: Springer, pp. 3–22.

Smith, L. (2006). *Uses of Heritage*. Abingdon: Routledge.

Springer, J. and Weiss, E. (2021). Responding to Claims of Archaeological Racism. *National Association of Scholars*. www.nas.org/blogs/article/responding-to-claims-of-archaeological-racism.

Stein, D. L. (2018). *The Hegemony of Heritage: Ritual and the Record in Stone*. Berkeley: University of California Press.

Stovel, H. (2008). Conserving the Sacred: Special Challenges for World Heritage Sites. *World Heritage Review*, **51**, 26–33.

Stovel, H., Stanley-Price, N., and Killick, R. (2005). Conservation of Living Religious Heritage. *Papers from the ICCROM 2003 Forum on Living Religious Heritage: Conserving the Sacred*. Rome.

Strausberg, M. (2011). *Religion and Tourism: Crossroads, Destinations and Encounters*. Abingdon: Routledge.

Sullivan, B. M. (2015). Introduction to Sacred Objects in Secular Spaces: Exhibiting Asian Religions in Museums. In B. M. Sullivan, ed., *Sacred Objects in Secular Spaces: Exhibiting Asian Religions in Museums*. London: Bloomsbury, pp. 1–6.

Tallett, F. and Atkin, N. (1991). Dechristianizing France: The Year II and the Revolutionary Experience. In Tallet. F., ed., *Religion, Society and Politics in France since 1789*. London and Rio Grande: The Hambledon Press, pp. 1–28.

Tanyieri-Erdemir, T. (2015). Historical Trajectories, Institutional Particularities: The Funding Regime for Religious Heritage in Turkey. In A. Fornerod, ed., *Funding Religious Heritage*. Farnham: Ashgate, pp. 213–226.

Teryukova, E. (2014). Display of Religious Objects in a Museum Space: Russian Museum Experience in the 1920s and 1930s. *Material Religion: The Journal of Objects, Art and Belief*, **10**(2), 255–258.

Tolia-Kelly, D. P, Waterton, E., and Watson, S. (2016). Introduction: Heritage, Affect and Emotion. In D. P. Tolia-Kelly, E. Waterton, and S. Watson, eds., *Heritage, Affect and Emotion*. Abingdon and New York: Routledge, pp. 1–11.

Trivedi, M. (2019). On Taking from Others: History and Sensibility in Archaeologists' Arguments for Treasure Trove Legislation. *Public Archaeology*, **17**(2/3), 1–27.

Tsivolas, T. (2019). The Legal Foundations of Religious Cultural Heritage Protection. *Religions*, **10**, 283.

Tuan, Y. F. (1989). *Space and Place: The Perspective of Experience*. Minneapolis: University of Minnesota Press.

Ucko, P. (1979). Review of AIAS Activities: 1978. *Australian Institute of Aboriginal Studies Newsletter*, **11**, 6–26.

Ucko, P. (1994). Foreword. In D. Carmichael, J. Hubert, B. Reeves, and A. Schanche, eds., *Sacred Sites, Sacred Places*. Abingdon: Routledge, pp. xiii–xxiii

Ugolnik, Z. (2016). Names Matter: How to Better Represent the Orthodox Churches in Textbooks and the Academy. *The Journal of Religion*, **96**(4), 506–543.

UNESCO (1949). *Human Rights: Comments and Interpretations*. New York: Columbia University Press.

UNESCO (1972). *Convention Concerning the Protection of the World Cultural and Natural Heritage, November 16, 1972*. UNESCO archives, file reference: WHC-2004/WS/2.

UNESCO (1989). Recommendation of the Safeguarding of Traditional Culture and Folklore. In *Records of the General Conference 25th Session October 17–November 16*. Paris, pp. 238–243.

UNESCO (1994). *Global Strategy for a Representative, Balanced and Credible World Heritage List*. https://whc.unesco.org/en/globalstrategy.

UNESCO (1996). *World Heritage Committee, Nineteenth session, Berlin, Germany, 1995*. UNESCO archives, file reference: WHC-95/CONF.203/21.

UNESCO (2003a). *Convention for the Safeguarding of the Intangible Cultural Heritage*. UNESCO archives, file reference: MISC/2003/CLT/CH/14.

UNESCO (2003b). *Compilation of Amendments from Member States Concerning the Convention for the Safeguarding of the Intangible Cultural Heritage*. UNESCO archives, file reference: CLT-2002/CONF.203/3 Rev.

UNESCO (2005). *Summary Record of the 29th Session of the World Heritage Committee, Durban South Africa*. UNESCO archives, file reference: WHC-05/20.COM/INF.22.

UNESCO (2010). *World Heritage Centre – Initiative on Heritage of Religious Interest*. http://whc.unesco.org/en/religious-sacred-heritage/.

UNESCO (2019). *Operational Guidelines for the Implementation of the World Heritage Convention*. UNESCO archives, file reference: WHC.19/01.

Valderrama, F. (1995). *A History of UNESCO*. Paris: UNESCO.

Vikan, G. (2017). Why U.S. Museums and the Antiquities Trade Should Work Together. *Apollo: The International Art Magazine*. www.apollo-magazine.com/antiquities-trade-us-museum-collecting-complex/.

Wade, L. (2021). An Archaeology Society Hosted a Talk against Returning Indigenous Remains. Some Want a New Society. *Science*. www.sciencemag.org/news/2021/04/archaeology-society-hosted-talk-against-returning-indigenous-remains-some-want-new. http://doi.org/10.1126/science.abj0843.

Warrack, S. (2011). Learning from Local Leaders: Working Together Toward the Conservation of Living Heritage at Angkor Wat, Cambodia. *Change Over Time*, **1**(1), 34–51.

Wei, C. and Aass, A. (1989). Heritage Conservation: East and West. *ICOMOS Information*, **3**, 3–8.

Weiss, E. and Springer, J. W. (2020). *Repatriation and Erasing the Past*. Gainesville: University of Florida Press.

Wild, R. and McLeod, C. (2008). *Sacred Natural Sites. Guidelines for Protected Area Managers*. Gland, Switzerland, and Paris: IUCN.

Winter, T. (2007). Heritage on the Margins. *Historic Environment. Special Issue "Places on the Margin,"* **20**(2), 2–7.

Zekrgoo, A. H. and Barkeshli, M. (2005). Collection Management of Islamic Heritage in Accordance with the Worldview and Shari'ah of Islam. In H. Stovel, N. Stanley-Price, and R. Killick, eds., *Conservation of Living Religious Heritage: Papers from the ICCROM 2003 Forum on Living Religious Heritage: Conserving the Sacred*, Rome: ICCROM3, pp. 94–101.

Zeruvabel, E. (2018). *Taken for Granted: The Remarkable Power of the Unremarkable*. Princeton: Princeton University Press.

Zhu, Y. (2020). Heritage and Religion in China. In S. Feutchtwang, ed., *Handbook on Religion in Contemporary China*. Cheltenham: Edward Elgar, pp. 96–108.

Zhu, Y., Wang, S., and Rowlands, M. (2020). Heritage and Religion in East Asia. In S. Wang, M. Rowlands, and Y. Zhu, eds., *Heritage and Religion in East Asia*. London: Routledge, pp. 1–12.

Acknowledgments

This Element was completed during a residential fellowship at the Center for Advanced Study in the Behavioral Sciences of Stanford University, supported by a Burkhardt Residential Fellowship for Recently Tenured Scholars from the American Council of Learned Societies. The discussions in this Element would not be possible without the foundational work of two incredible colleagues and mentors: Denis Byrne and Anna Karlström. I am grateful to Liz Roberts and Sharon Block for helping me structure this manuscript and Sam Holley-Kline, Sabrina Papazian, Victoria Ramenzoni, Liz Marlowe, Fiona Greenland, and Jonah Siegel for commenting on earlier versions. Finally, I thank Shanon Fitzpatrick and Vincent Tornabene for their editorial support.

Cambridge Elements ☰

Critical Heritage Studies

Kristian Kristiansen
University of Gothenburg

Michael Rowlands
UCL

Francis Nyamnjoh
University of Cape Town

Astrid Swenson
Bath University

Shu-Li Wang
Academia Sinica

Ola Wetterberg
University of Gothenburg

About the Series

This series focuses on the recently established field of Critical Heritage Studies.
Interdisciplinary in character, it brings together contributions from experts working in
a range of fields, including cultural management, anthropology, archaeology, politics,
and law. The series will include volumes that demonstrate the impact of contemporary
theoretical discourses on heritage found throughout the world, raising awareness of the
acute relevance of critically analysing and understanding the way heritage is used today
to form new futures.

Cambridge Elements ⁼

Critical Heritage Studies

9 781009 183598